PRAISE F
KINDRED CREATION

"The parables in *Kindred Creation* show us the light on the walk of life."

— NIKKI GIOVANNI, poet, author and seven-time NAACP Image Award
winner

"This book is a masterpiece! Drawing from the best parts of our traditions,
Kindred Creation is an offering of high art, radical political philosophy, and spiritual nourishment. Aida Mariam Davis has gifted us with a text that not only
spotlights and challenges lingering colonial logics, but also provides theories,
tools, and tactics that are necessary for audacious freedom, dreaming, and
courageous worldmaking. Read this book and prepare to be unsettled, challenged,
inspired, and healed."

— MARC LAMONT HILL, author and BET News correspondent

"Writer, leader, visionary, and storyteller, Aida Mariam Davis has turned centuries of accumulated knowledge and wisdom from the victims of settler colonialism into a lyrical, audacious appeal to decolonize everything in order to
preserve and repair our planet. A vital contribution that needs to be translated
into every language."

— ROBIN D. G. KELLEY, author of *Freedom Dreams*

"*Kindred Creation* is an invitation to rip colonial borders out of our hearts and souls
by the roots, and then rebuild, restore, and reimagine what lives lived together
could look like. A future built on the ancient, collective roots of trees and relatives
that have never stopped reaching toward us. It is an invitation to be made whole."

— PATTY KRAWEC, cohost of the *Medicine for the Resistance* podcast, cofounder
of the Nii'kinaaganaa Foundation, and author of *Becoming Kin*

"Here, Aida Mariam Davis presents the possibilities of dismantling settler colonial systems within design by imagining how Black and Indigenous belief systems, kinship, and solidarity will help us imagine new ways of being and belonging in the world. With its poetic style and rhythmic writing that only a Black woman can produce, *Kindred Creation* moves us in the direction toward decolonial futures in ways we didn't know we needed . . . this book is a must-read!"

> —KYLE T. MAYS, PhD, associate professor in the departments of African American studies, American Indian studies, and history at UCLA and author of *An Afro-Indigenous History of the United States*

"This book is a marvel because it gives us a nonlinear, contrapuntal, and ancient-yet-contemporary way of comprehending the social and the wider world of today that can inspire a viable revolutionary praxis of tomorrow. As part of the storied legacy of African decolonizing and postcolonial writing, Aida Mariam Davis has given us a visionary's insights into how the African diaspora and its complexly oppressive origins and history have, indeed, sown the seeds of radical emancipatory transformation of the modern world in our moment. Though this book compels us to reflect deeply, it just may be the spark needed to also compel serious transformative action."

> —DANIEL O. SAYERS, author of *A Desolate Place for a Defiant People* and *Enslaved Laborers in the Great Dismal Swamp*

"In *Kindred Creation*, Aida Mariam Davis offers timeless wisdom to combat our most pernicious ills. In this era of rising individual and geopolitical isolation, Davis insists on the importance of collective work and vision, and on the centrality of Black and Indigenous communal ties and traditions. *Kindred Creation* is clear-sighted and precise, heart-centered and expansive. A balm."

> —ANGELA FLOURNOY, author of the *New York Times* Notable Book *The Turner House*

"This book is a powerful testimony to the richness of African and Black knowledges. Both inspiring and poignant, Davis takes an incisive look at the past and invites us to reclaim our interconnectedness. A must-read!"

> —ANNA TUBBS, author of the *New York Times* best seller *Three Mothers*

"*Kindred Creation* is both a revival and a revelation. Davis connects us to ourselves and reminds us of our spiritual inheritance as Black people. Deeply concerned with our interconnectedness and renewal, *Kindred Creation* shows us the magic, majesty, and magnificence that is Blackness. A must-read for anyone working to create a future worthy of our children."

—MICHAEL TUBBS, special advisor for economic mobility to California Governor Gavin Newsom and former mayor of Stockton

"All of nature, of which humans are a small part, is sentient. This precious book reminds us that if we, humans, refuse to acknowledge our individual and collective responsibility in caring for the earth and all beings on it, it is at our own peril. Love is the answer to every question."

—ERICKA HUGGINS, author of *Comrade Sister*

"*Kindred Creation* is in the family way with languages, musings, musicalities, worldviews, ontologies, epistemologies, and axiologies of free and ancient futures."

—FANIA DAVIS, civil rights attorney and restorative justice practitioner

"I'm so glad our children are growing up in a world where this book exists. This is a must-read for all schools and for parents of Black children who can use Aida's smart, decolonized lens as a tool to reimagine/create a revolutionary new world of freedom."

—JESSICA MCKAY, *New York Times* best-selling author of *Always with You, Always with Me* and educator

"If America is to become a flourishing multiracial democracy where all can participate, prosper, and reach their full potential, it must realize that its path to an equitable future is inextricably linked to the people that this country has never loved. The soulful traditions of Blackness and indigeneity provide a path forward where this nation is compelled to see the humanity of all who reside here and to work in service of their thriving. Aida's vision and voice are seminal and represent the leadership necessary to unlock the promise of the nation by unleashing the promise in us all."

—DR. MICHAEL MCAFEE, president and CEO of PolicyLink

"The American experiment in democracy may be nearly 250 years old, but our attempt to realize a multiracial and pluralistic society of free and equal citizens has yet to be born. Aida Mariam Davis's clarion call in *Kindred Creation* reminds us that we must look backward to reclaim and repair in order to chart any path forward."

—ROB REICH, author of *Just Giving* and professor of political science at Stanford University

KINDRED CREATION

KINDRED CREATION

PARABLES AND PARADIGMS FOR FREEDOM

AIDA MARIAM DAVIS

Foreword by ANGELA Y. DAVIS

North Atlantic Books

Huichin, unceded Ohlone land
Berkeley, California

Published by
North Atlantic Books
Huichin, unceded Ohlone land
Berkeley, California

Cover image © Paepaestockphoto via
 Getty Images
Cover art and design by Jasmine Hromjak
Book design by Happenstance Type-O-Rama

Printed in the United States of America

Kindred Creation: Parables and Paradigms for Freedom is sponsored and published by North Atlantic Books, an educational nonprofit based in the unceded Ohlone land Huichin (Berkeley, CA) that collaborates with partners to develop cross-cultural perspectives; nurture holistic views of art, science, the humanities, and healing; and seed personal and global transformation by publishing work on the relationship of body, spirit, and nature.

North Atlantic Books's publications are distributed to the US trade and internationally by Penguin Random House Publisher Services. For further information, visit our website at www.northatlanticbooks.com.

Library of Congress Cataloging-in-Publication Data

Names: Davis, Aida Mariam, author.
Title: Kindred creation : parables and paradigms for freedom / Aida Mariam
    Davis ; foreword by Angela Davis.
Description: Berkeley, California : North Atlantic Books, [2024] | Includes
    bibliographical references and index. | Summary: "An exploration of the
    historical and ongoing impacts of settler colonialism, and a call to
    design better worlds rooted in African lifeways"— Provided by
    publisher.
Identifiers: LCCN 2024017984 (print) | LCCN 2024017985 (ebook) | ISBN
    9798889841364 (trade paperback) | ISBN 9798889841371 (ebook)
Subjects: LCSH: Settler colonialism. | Decolonization. |
    Liberty—Philosophy. | Kinship. | Creation.
Classification: LCC JV105 (print) | LCC JV105 (ebook) | DDC
    325/.3—dc23/eng/20240821
LC record available at https://lccn.loc.gov/2024017984
LC ebook record available at https://lccn.loc.gov/2024017985

1 2 3 4 5 6 7 8 9 VERSA 29 28 27 26 25 24

For my family, the midwives of this book.

*To the courageous ones who never submitted
and to those who bear the weight of being
well—I honor and thank you.*

CONTENTS

FOREWORD

As the aunt of her future husband, I was invited by Aida Mariam to read the poem "Resignation" by Nikki Giovanni at their wedding, which was officiated by my sister Fania. "I love you/because the Earth turns around the sun/ because the North wind blows north." At the time I was honored but did not fully understand why she and my nephew had asked us, her affinal kin, to play such prominent roles in their marriage rites. It was not until some years (and three children) later, when I read her illuminative reflections in *Kindred Creation* that I began to more deeply appreciate Aida's motivations for positioning us in a ceremony that would inhabit their memory and would be shared with others for many years to come. Now, having read this book, I realize how central kindred creation is to her worldview, and how, even when this relationality appears to be given, it is actually always a creation of ongoing praxis.

As this book confirms, Aida is philosophically driven to shuttle between the smallest insight and its most immense implications. The trees she evokes at the center of one of her parables, for example, can only be deeply understood by being attentive to the communicative power of their roots, as many of us first learned from the Indigenous plant ecologist Robin Wall Kimmerer. For Aida Mariam Davis, the small fact is never treated as an isolated phenomenon— it is always an occasion for raising consequential questions and for identifying deep-rooted connections to something much larger. Take the selection of the wedding venue, for example. The choice of the old Southern Pacific Railroad Station on 16th street in Oakland, which dates back to 1912, was not based solely on its timeworn beauty and its Beaux-Arts architectural style. She and her husband chose it also and especially because it was one of the significant historical settings for the Brotherhood of Sleeping Car Porters, the first major Black labor union in the US, whose West Coast headquarters was there. Aida's characteristic attentiveness to the labor movement emanates not only from her political awareness of the need to acknowledge the central place of the labor movement in the constellation of our struggles for social justice, but also from her own work as a union organizer. There is an imperative here to be simultaneously attentive to the aesthetic dimension, political history, and the way personal trajectories often recapitulate the promise of beauty and what has come before. One of the many important paradigms evoked in this text is that struggles against racial capitalism are not to be siloed into a particular designated realm, but rather incorporated into all aspects of our lives in order to have a transformative effect on the ways we live.

For those of us who come to this text with a long history of struggle against racial capitalism, *Kindred Creation* presents us with a paradigm-shifting approach to revolutionary change. Instead of assuming that revolutionary transformation only flows from change in political leadership, or change in the structure of the state, we are asked to join in an urgent collective process of challenging settler colonialism. This opposition comes not only through challenging state violence as expressed through genocidal war against the people of Palestine, the continued assaults on Indigenous people in the Americas, and the still routine police murders of Black and brown people in the US and elsewhere, but also through attempting to change our ways of knowing, feeling, and being in the world. This also entails rehearsing trajectories that conceptually move us across oceans and continents and back to quotidian resistance practices that remind us to forge, along the way, new relations, new modes of kinship, and relationalities that reach beyond what we might consider our communities and also, as Aida always emphasizes, beyond the borders of the human. These parables and paradigms offer us deep connections with emancipatory strategies that are responsible for the fact that, despite the devastation brought about by racial capitalism, so many of us are still here, still attempting to heed the call for global justice.

—*Angela Y. Davis*

ACKNOWLEDGMENTS

Temesgen.

Black love will always be Black wealth. My beloved Reggie, thank you for inviting me home to myself and showing me the quiet strength of patience, passion, and perseverance; for allowing me to witness and experience the most remarkable parent and partner I've ever known; and for sharpening my iron by engaging all my intellectual and spiritual faculties.

And for the greatest gifts I've ever known—my children. You remind me that children are not in the way, they are the way. *Yene jegnaoch*, my heroes, you inspire all who encounter you to recall that our truest nature is to bloom. Thank you for reminding me that we first sing before we talk, dance before we walk, and draw before we write—that we are born artists. This book was written for, by, and because of you: whether I was pregnant, nursing, or thinking about you, you co-wrote this, and for that I venerate you.

I also want to acknowledge this precious planet we inhabit and her many gifts. Thank you, Mother Earth for East Oakland, South Los Angeles, Apple Valley, Baltimore, Berkeley, and the many places that deposited ideas and ideologies into my spirit. I want to appreciate the sacred soil of the Maroons to docks of the Montgomery River Brawl that remind us that rebellion and refuge are possible and within reach. I must also recognize the many nonhuman kin that offer me unconditional care and show me how to live life naturally in rhythm. I thank you, Mother Earth, importantly, for the cycles of life and circularity of time.

In the truest Black and African tradition, this project took a village. Whether they were loving on my babies so I could write, questioning my ideas, or encouraging me when I wanted to stop, they were reminding me *who I am, and whose I am.* I love and deeply appreciate my chosen family, namely Selena Wilson, Sharim Hannegan-Martinez, Robin D. G. Kelley, Anna Tubbs, Michael Tubbs, Ashleigh Ellis, Alicia Zakon, Lauren Baranco, Ime Archibong, Jessica McKay, Patty Krawec, Daniel Sayers, Andrea "Ms. Rochelle" Epps, Julia "Nana" Raspberry, Victoria Teshome, Nick Talarico, Celina Culver, Marcie Bianco, Julie Dragland, Alyse Killeen, Mabie Settledge, Dorothy Settledge, Aja Byrd, Héritier Lumumba, Kevin Bethune, Angela Flournoy, Nasim Fluker, Nikki Jourdain Earl, Kyle Mays, Michael McAfee, Lauryn Nwankpa, and Pastor Michael McBride.

And to my blood family—Abigail Mariam, James Ramsey, Mesrak Gessesse, Alemayehu Mariam, Alexandra "Buttons" Gessesse, Menasse Gessesse, Beirut Gessesse, Alexandra Hazandrea, Gina Dent, Angela Y. Davis, Reginald Davis Sr., Fania Davis, Matthew Gessesse, Alia Peera, Esete "Kiddy" Getachew, David Getachew Smith Jr.—you are so deeply appreciated.

I am also deeply indebted to the many brilliant and caring people at North Atlantic Books who understood the potential of this book and worked tirelessly to maintain its integrity. To my literary agent Dana Newman whose commitment to this project was steadfast and righteous. To my editor Jasmine Respess who encouraged my most radical vision and channeled Toni Morrison's editing into this text. And a tremendous thank you to my production editor Janelle Ludowise who met this project with intense care and faithfully kept the spirit of this book, at all costs. This circle of complete intellectual care and support was my lifeline when others attempted to diminish and dismiss the ideas in this book.

Lastly, I am thankful for ancestral African wisdom; both embodied and oral lore. Especially for this Yoruba one: the ram that moves backward does so to bring more power.

Ase!

The Flowering Mimosa

My elders tell stories to share supernatural wisdom. They spoke to me in a dream and shared the testimony of the mimosa tree:

Torrential rains are common this time of year. Springtime represents the renewal and rebirth of all beings, especially trees. Acacias gossip and giggle with the baobabs, sharing the talk of the village. Meanwhile, the wispy flowering magenta mimosa tree sings songs of struggle and joy every morning, rain or shine.

Pregnant with the possibility of the generations of trees to follow, the mimosa gleefully greets every child who passes as she knows they will one day inherit her. She is a part of an above-ground tribe of sun-loving trees that speaks their minds and keeps the sacred village stories. Her daily labor is valued by the village people. She, along with the other trees and organisms, is a part of an underground network that labors together to replenish and regenerate the Earth.

Once, years ago, visitors came to the village. Their essence was very strange: they never spoke to the trees or plants, they built their own homes where village huts stood, and they brought fire to the ground. Those visitors ignored, even attempted to destroy, the mimosa tree's beauty and her ability to offer songs, shade, and sustenance to the community. Much of the damage caused by the visitors was visible, but there was also damage that was invisible. To repair and restore herself, she replanted.

Despite that scarring encounter, the mimosa is surprised to learn that the ground is actually more fertile after a fire and that she remains unchanged in her divine purpose—to bloom. She plans to share this lesson, along with many others, with every seed she produces for generations to come.

Rooted in deep and sororal kinship, trees reveal our deepest truths about living fully and freely. For millennia, African and other Indigenous cultures have acknowledged and been in awe of the way trees change, connect, and communicate. Trees, like all organisms, live, breathe, speak, and self-organize. They live with their dead: the outer sections of the tree are alive with cells transporting water and sugar, but the core of the trunk is dead. Particular trees, like the baobab, possess spirits that are powerful forces to guide decision-making. This understanding and reverence for trees is in stark contrast to settler logic.

Until recently, Western scientists claimed that trees and other plants could not communicate because they did not possess the same speaking faculties as humans or other animals. Scientists only understood the potential for plants to communicate purely through the lens of human capacity. Their reluctance to explore the intricate nature of trees demonstrates, on one hand, a kind of human superiority to all other organisms and, on the other, a lack of curiosity or interest in learning from other cultures. Western scientists' recent "discovery" that trees communicate has been hailed as a revolution of scientific understanding. This pattern of the powerful asserting themselves as the sole authority and arbiter of what is "real," while denying the decades of Indigenous wisdom is desecration. This "revelation" demonstrates a refusal to engage or acknowledge the past and present experience of interconnectedness as told by Indigenous peoples around the world.

Trees, flowers, and gardens offer us beauty and complexity that give meaning to our lives, but more importantly, these nonhuman kin give us breathing space to experience grace, the unmerited favor from the divine. As we travel together, narrator and reader, let us not follow the path of the sanctimonious scientist and dismiss ancestral wisdom. Instead, let us be reminded of the role and responsibility we have to steward the land, recall and realize the language of those who've come before, and recognize the interconnected nature of our lifestyle. With this awareness, we can create with intention and care for generations to come.

INTRODUCTION TO KINDRED CREATION

You measure a people's potential for liberation based on how different their culture is from their oppressors.
—AMÍLCAR CABRAL, engineer, political organizer, and diplomat; from *National Liberation and Culture*

Who taught you to love yourself? Who taught you to love the texture of your hair, the shape of your nose, the deep color of your skin? Who taught you to love your people?

The answers to these questions are where we start our journey together. You and I are defined by beginnings and endings—how we start, stagnate, or submit to the world around us. The courage to begin again exposes our own power and potential. Something deep within you wants to release the status quo and the stagnation of sameness for a life of creation and kinship.

In many ways, this book is akin to a quilt. It is an intentional assemblage of discarded pieces stitched together to evoke African mud cloth patterns and reveal embedded hidden messages. Created to celebrate heritage and bring warmth, quilts have historically been covers and comforters for displaced Africans, offering them solace and inspiration as they rebuild, re-create, and reclaim themselves in spite of hardship. We take scraps and make masterpieces. I submit to you that this is a quilt of poetry, prophecy, and philosophy, where pain is transformed into power and power turns into generational practice.

We, the descendants of Africans, are here to define ourselves for ourselves. We do not allow our existence to be defined by and understood by Eurocentric paradigms and value systems. This book is not created for the settler way of life. This text is not for settler consumption, nor will it make sense to the settler colonial context. Instead, it will require you and I to reclaim African and Indigenous belief systems to create new worlds and new relationships. Which is why this book is as much about creation as it is about kinship. Everything we encounter, experience, and endure is designed. Despite design's ubiquity as a concept, its definitional dilemma remains. Understanding the role of design within the settler colonial context is both complex and circumstantial. All creatures, from bees to humans, possess the potential and power to change and create the conditions of the world around us.

So much has been taken from Black, African, and Indigenous people in settler colonialism. But not all was lost. Decolonization is both absence and presence: the absence of violence, erasure, and settler status quo; and the presence of kinship, responsibility, and imagination. For the purposes of this text, I define *decolonization* as the personal and political resistance to the forced relationship of bondage and exploitation of the colonized to the colonizer. Recently, decolonization has become a buzzword and a metaphor to suggest reform in a variety of sectors to create a better world. This is a misnomer of settler colonization. True decolonization amounts to collective freedom work.

In *The Wretched of the Earth*, philosopher Frantz Fanon wrote, "decolonization, which sets out to change the order of the world, is a programme of complete disorder" requiring complete release of the native-slave-settler relationship. Tactically, it requires the disruptive rematriation of the land, lifestyle, and language to Black and Indigenous peoples internationally.

Those people and places that have been or are currently being colonized are not a monolith. Instead, we are a constellation of distinct, yet connected, entities. I offer my lived experience as a Black, African woman throughout this text to demonstrate the personal impacts of colonization and to reject the settler colonial pattern of compartmentalizing and commodifying ourselves for comfortable consumption. The experiences represented in this text are careful not to define people by colonization, but rather to present opportunities to learn and create solidarity and kinship based on lived experiences, ancestral wisdom, and radical imagination.

Children of Africans who were stolen from Africa and enslaved in the Americas are no less African than the Africans left behind in Africa and made victims of European colonialism. To be stolen from your mother does not make you any less her child or any less a member of the family. Socialization and indoctrination can make you believe that you are not connected to your own mother. Africans on the continent and Africans throughout the diaspora must understand the power of recognizing that we have one mother who originates in Africa. Additionally, we must understand both the common core of African *beingness* and the divergent and varied expressions of African experiences. For too long, the connection between Black people has been complex given our history of enslavement, separation, and suspicion. But still, our kinship has flourished in spite of settler violence.

Black* people around the world represent freedom. To be Black is to be endowed with emancipatory vision filled with possibilities beyond the world we occupy. A world that sees the fullness of our people and planet. I recognize the many manifestations of anti-Blackness, misogynoir, ableism, and transphobia globally, as well as within African and Indigenous communities, and I am intentionally choosing to address this book to the oppressed of the world, starting with those Black people on the periphery. Also, it is not lost on me that Black people can and do end up becoming oppressors and junior partners of colonial and neocolonial systems. Black people who represent settler power and oppression are, for all intents and purposes, considered representatives and victims of the oppressors. I exalt the voices that have been erased, denied, or otherwise unrecorded by sharing some of their vision and stories here.

Design, like decolonization, has become a buzzword without one definition. So that we have a shared understanding, I submit to you that design is

---

* A note on terminology: I use *African* and *Black* as well as *Indigenous* and *Native* interchangeably in the text for shorthand purposes. I acknowledge the important distinctions and nuances and invite correction by members of respective groups.

a reflection of how we feel about people. Design is one of the most potent forces in our lives. Whether by action or inaction, how we live, where we live, and even how long we live are manifestations of design. Design communicates our values, vision, and voice. In the practice of design, we can be reminded of our potential, purpose, and beauty. More important than the outcomes of design is the process—the small and everyday movements. The activity of considering and creating our world allows us to create new connections between ideas, people, and our environment.

Beyond the tactical and practical approaches of design lies the concept of *creation*. This is the idea that we can care, nurture, and develop the spirit in people and the planet. Creation mandatorily means bringing something to life. Often that new life breaks binaries and builds bridges. Design, in its many definitions, has meant relating to or reflecting settler dominant values. *Kindred Creation* is not about reforming or decolonizing design, it is about reclaiming who we are (and who we've always been) without the imposition of settler society, and it is about stewarding African Indigenous cultural practices and wisdoms. The journey of creation is the practice and pursuit of sovereignty and self-determination by remembering the past, resisting the status quo, reclaiming ourselves, and remaking the world. *Kindred Creation* goes radically to the root to understand circumstances, create new kin, study and struggle together, and most importantly, care for each other's spiritual development—in short it is about love.

The connections and the subsequent responsibilities to those entities, human and nonhuman, amount to what Africans call *kinship*. African-centered philosophy offers the idea of kinship as an alternative to the dominant mythology that reform is the only way to create ourselves, our communities, and our world. In this way kinship honors the multitudinous ways of knowing, being, and doing to envision and create a full and fair future. For readers who are not Black, it can be tempting to look for analogous elements of the African experience shared here and assign them to your own way of being. Resist that impulse. Instead, identify the ways settler colonization and oppression have become a transnational condition. One that impacts the social, political, economic, and spiritual well-being of all that it touches. Let us understand our past and present differences to build meaningful solidarity.

In this book, I enlist the wisdom, wit, and brilliance of my kin. I've invited fictive, chosen, and blood kin to a conversation on re-creating relationships. Spanning matters of death and rebirth, destruction and creation, this book is my perspective on our collective genealogy as Black people around the world. This is *not* a book of solutions. Organized in three parts, the goal of the book is to operate as a philosophical guide for Black and oppressed peoples to reclaim freedom through kinship and creation.

"Part I—Re-member: The Routes and Roots of Settler Colonialism" unforgets the unending and cascading violence of settler colonialism and other forms of domination. This section explores land, language, lifestyle, and labor—how settler colonialism has been and continues to be the primary driver of historical and ongoing dehumanization, death, and destruction. In addition to the terror and trauma of colonialism, we explore the suffocating impacts and deadly distraction forgetting poses to the important labor of creating new, regenerative life. And yet, more than accepting the history provided by settlers, we can retell our own history, our way. By recalling the heritage and history of the oppressed we reclaim history, as told by the hostages.

"Part II—Refuse: Unsettle the Settler" outlines how we individually, interpersonally, and institutionally refuse and resist death-making institutions and relationships. Resisting and rejecting the cascading effects of colonization has been an intergenerational struggle for Black and Indigenous people. While this text is rooted in the community and kinship of my personal life and work, I explore everyday ways we can choose kinship and self-determination in spite of our current conditions and ongoing violence. "Refuse" explores nourishing and fulfilling forms of insubordination as well as ways of being that affirm our own dignity and that of all creatures.

"Part III—Reclaim: Return to Right Relationship" reveals the fact that freedom is with us and within reach. In this, the most personal section of the book, I offer how you can consider birthing a new world and new relationships, a world where we are completely free and recentered on kinship. Recalling the themes in Part I, here we revisit and reclaim land, language, lifestyle, and labor on Black terms. I offer us archiving, storytelling, and mutual aid—prototypes of new ways to create and connect based on our African beingness.

Kindred Creation transcends the status quo in its physical design and discourse. By excavating some of the erased and stolen voices, I aim to poetically reclaim and celebrate the humanity and lifestyle of those who have been reduced to marginalized peoples and deliver a vision for realizing Black people's dignity and distinction. The physical structure of this text is designed to embed remembrance, resistance, and reclamation through narratives, fiction, poems, parables, allegories, songs, conversations, theories, memories, prompts, prophecies, and curiosities. It is a call and response. My hope is that you holler, sing, and dance to the words here.

My writing is intentionally integrated, feminist, polyglot, and mobile. Shifting between time and place, academic and colloquial, Amharic, English, and AAVE (African-American Vernacular English) languages, is intentional, designed to create a text in motion that unsettles our relationship to language as we know it. I employ African and other Indigenous ways of knowing, sharing, and being to be a testimony to the richness of our way of life and our unique and often unnoticed knowledge systems. This book is interested in the unseen: the things that conspire to keep people and the planet proximate to their power and potential.

Though I have attended notable universities, received a great deal of formal education, and held influential roles at a variety of organizations, I resist the socialization to internalize that as a validating and legitimizing experience for ideas in this book. Rather, I recall the difficulties and struggles I encountered as a Black woman in those spaces as inspiration for creating new learning experiences. The life lessons I have learned animate my vision and energize me to create alternative perspectives anchored in the Black and Indigenous knowledge, culture, spiritual traditions, and imagination.

The undertaking of this book is not academic or theoretical for me. I am a descendant of anticolonial fighters who kept Ethiopia free from colonialism when virtually all of Africa was carved out and divided among European powers. My great-grandfather fought in the Battle of Adwa in 1896, in which the Italian colonial army was defeated by Ethiopian warriors in less than twenty-four hours, marking the first time in documented history that a Black army decisively defeated and routed a modern and well-equipped European army.

My grandfather fought in the Ethiopian resistance after the Italians invaded Ethiopia in 1935. He was captured and interned in a concentration camp called Danane in Italian Somaliland for five years. I have an intergenerational inheritance of embodied wisdom, vision, and activism. I was taught an Ethiopian proverb, "If the silk of spiders' webs could be united, they can tie up a lion." The practical life lesson of this proverb is that if people under settler colonialism bind together, they can liberate themselves. For generations, Black and Indigenous people employed these kinds of allegories to teach, learn, inspire, and know.

From East Oakland to South LA to East Africa, I have worked on countless community campaigns to cultivate and sustain movements that realize working peoples' highest potential and power. As a long-time community organizer-turned-founder of the organization Decolonize Design, I am able to connect theory and praxis in untraditional and distinct ways. Integral to movement-building are alternative ways of knowing and being that are not rooted in dominant culture and transactional processes; instead they are rooted in deep relational efforts that speak to our universal sacred personhood.

For centuries, Black people have witnessed and experienced violent cycles of failed reforms and redesigns of fundamentally colonial institutions that create ongoing intergenerational harm. Whether we acknowledge it or not, we are all impacted and limited by these systems of oppression. We, Black and African people, are reclaiming our vision and voice to create a world and future beyond surviving, beyond assimilation—a world and future of intergenerational joy and freedom for us all.

Lastly, this book belongs to you. It longs to be with you and it is yours to use to remind you that we are not separate and yet we are not the same. You were always free—never forget that.

Let us begin.

Definitions belonged to the definers, not the defined.

—TONI MORRISON, *Beloved*

PART I

RE-MEMBER

THE ROUTES AND ROOTS OF SETTLER COLONIALISM

Sankofa

se wo were fi na wosan kofa a yenki

Translation: It is not taboo to go back and fetch what you forgot.

The adinkra symbol of *Sankofa* is visually represented by a mythical bird, standing with its body forward facing, feet firmly planted on the soil, its head turned backward, holding an egg in its mouth. Symbolically, this image shows us our hearts' desire to move forward, our heads' desire to remember, and the fertility and possibility of the future as represented by the egg. Sankofa reminds us that we must go back in order to move forward. The act of remembering and recalling is important as a first step to reclamation and re-creation.

In this part we will explore the multilayered meanings of stories, words, and folk sayings in African diaspora communities through their knowledge and lived experiences. In community, we can draw inspiration and lessons from the past to transform our experience today. I invite you to reconsider how you recall the past. I submit to you, *re-membering* is a special kind *re-collection*, where people who share a life story come together to collect the past. In doing so, we can reclaim our sense of self, status, and power and,

more importantly, our intuition, identity, and imagination. The hyphen-
ation in re-member is deliberate to demonstrate the word's primary role—to
bring together the members or people of the event or experience being
recalled. Through the process of *re-membering*, we can recover and build
rituals and ceremonies of togetherness in the present. We understand our
world, and ourselves, through relationships, past and present.

For too long, designers, and creators, have subscribed to *methodolatry*—the
strict adherence to a set of methods despite ever-changing environments, new
information, intuition, or interpretation. As a result, settler society has hin-
dered new discoveries. By worshiping a particular method, we promote the
binary, or set of offered options, and anything outside of our classifications
becomes irrelevant or forgotten. We are asked to focus on the present and
practical at the expense and erasure of others. By design, the settler colonial
project has denied the intensely interconnected nature of our relationships.
Re-membering is uniting the members of a family—past, present, and future—
creating new relatives and kin, human and nonhuman alike. Only then can
we collectively imagine ways and worlds that aren't born yet. Aimé Césaire,
the poet and father of the Negritude movement, tells us that no one colonizes
innocently or without impunity; rather, a nation that colonizes is a sick,
morally diseased civilization. The Negritude movement was an anticolonial,
political, and cultural movement led by African and Caribbean students in
the 1930s to reclaim the beauty and brilliance of Blackness.

Colonizing nations are not just metaphorically diseased; these nations
brought pandemics and plagues to African civilizations and Indigenous
populations. Over generations, settler colonization results in epigenetic
and traumagenic damage and suffering that is complex, continuous, com-
pounding, collective, and cumulative. From smallpox and the bubonic
plague to hypertension and diabetes, the disease and devastation inflicted
by colonization has manifested in the form of sexual violence, chronic dis-
eases, addiction, abject poverty, and high suicide rates, among other adverse
health outcomes. At an individual level, settler colonialism erodes the emotional, spiritual, intellectual, physical, and social sense of self-regard. To
add insult to injury, the settler colonial project responds to this trauma as an
impediment to economic growth and development. Settler colonial systems

are designed to destroy or assimilate those who dare assert their humanity, not to repair the harm or respond with care.

Settler colonization has been (and continues to be) a critical public health crisis while it places a heavy burden on the mental, physical, emotional, and spiritual health of the colonized. The genocide of Native peoples and the enslavement of Native Americans, followed by the kidnapping and enslavement of Africans, and the denial of ongoing violence, all rely on the erasure and invisibility of displaced and exploited peoples.

Colonizing nations' obstinate refusal to remember the past is a failure to connect the historical trauma of colonization to its long and cascading impacts. Most importantly, settler colonialism has changed how we all understand ourselves, both settler and colonized, and it has corrupted what it is to be healthy and to be in a respectful relationship with the land and other creatures. Recovering the health, well-being, and humanity of oppressed peoples depends on remembering, acknowledging, and addressing historical and ongoing forms of settler colonization.

Black feminist thinkers, like my college professor the late VèVè Clark, give us vision and language to push for even more than the New Negro, Indigenist, and Negritude movements and explore the past from the perspective of regional, ethnic, and peasant experiences, calling out the distinct cultural repression. Remembering that settler colonization is a journey that requires us to explore the terror and trauma of our past and present as well as unlearn and question every aspect of what we think we know. To guide us on this journey, I've invited elders, ancestors, activists, thinkers, and children to help make meaning and share alternative ways of knowing. We will explore the realities and lived experiences of the oppressed under settler colonialism as a distinct form of colonization in order to uncover its past and present characteristics and contexts.

From Bahia's shores of Brazil to Charleston, South Carolina to Ouidah, Benin—colonization is the intergenerational experience of brutal subjugation, sexual violence, appropriation, domination, genocide, and everyday abuse and assaults.

Settler colonialism is an ongoing sociopolitical-economic system created by European nations that perpetuate the settler occupation, deliberate displacement, destruction, repression, erasure, and exploitation of African and Indigenous peoples and cultures worldwide. Together with anti-Blackness, heteropatriarchy, ableism, and capitalism, settler colonialism forms an interlocking oppression that normalizes settler occupation and complete exploitation. Though not identical in every context or country, settler colonization globally shares many of these key features.

Yet despite the many independence declarations from African and other Indigenous nations, settler colonization continues on because it employs a Eurocentric doctrine of ethnic, moral, and natural superiority to reinforce these values and normalize the settler occupation and displacement as inevitable. This mode of oppression remains the root cause for much of the injustice, violence, and dehumanization descendants of the colonized experience today. For the purposes of this text, we will remember settler colonialism by exploring the impact on land, language, lifestyle, and labor. Though not exhaustive or mutually exclusive, remembering will be our starting point to recall colonization's implications as a past and present experience.

LAND

The land knows you, even when you are lost.
—ROBIN WALL KIMMERER, *Braiding Sweetgrass*

Land is the basis of all independence. Land is the basis of freedom, justice, and equality.
—MALCOLM X, "Message to the Grass Roots," Northern Negro Grass Roots Leadership Conference, Detroit, November 1963

The full rematriation of land to African and Indigenous peoples around the world is the most urgent and tangible demand of decolonization. Children, culture, customs—all have been stripped away and stolen as communities have fought to survive and maintain stewardship of the land of their ancestors. Too often in colonial and capitalistic contexts we understand the theft of land as the loss of property or capital. It is critical to note the inextricable and mutually reinforcing nature of colonialism and capitalism. Colonization paved the way for capitalism through the exploitation of forced labor and the natural resources of stolen land. As an African, I know the land always belonged to itself; it could never be bought or sold.

African and other Indigenous peoples have long been protectors of land, water, air, and wildlife. For millennia these people fought to maintain harmony in nature and sustain biodiversity and ecosystems because they knew the purpose of the land was to be regenerative for generations to come. Despite oppression and displacement, African and other Indigenous peoples knew this wisdom and brought it with them through time and place. Whether it was their homeland, in the Native American context, or the new land forced upon them, in the case of kidnapped enslaved Africans, land held in community gave people strength; it gave them something to fight for.

Native American activist and economist Winona LaDuke explains the importance of land and food in its relationship to sustaining our complete health and well-being in her book *Recovering the Sacred: The Power of Naming and Claiming*:

> The recovery of the people is tied to the recovery of food, since food itself is medicine: not only for the body, but for the soul, for the spiritual connection to history, ancestors, and the land.

The loss of traditional foodways is a loss of nutrition and medicine for our physical, mental, and emotional selves. Our individual wellness cannot be separated from the land that produces so much of what we depend on to be healthy and whole. This is a dramatic juxtaposition to the settler colonial logic of exploiting and extracting from the land for economic and labor interests.

Settlers, by definition, require that people be displaced through settlements and elimination. In an article entitled "The Rest of Us: Rethinking Settler and Native," historian and scholar Robin D. G. Kelley points out that the African encounter with settler colonialism was primarily marked by exploitative processes such as labor regimes. The extractive arrangements were often the very mechanisms that oppressed Indigenous peoples of their lands. He demonstrates that in the cases of enslaved Africans in America and in South Africa and the construction of white settler social relations in the country "the expropriation of the native from the land was a fundamental objective, but so was proletarianization." They wanted the land and the labor, but not the people—that is to say, they sought to eliminate stable communities and their cultures of resistance.

The attempted elimination of collective and sacred personhood, Kelley shows, is a political goal pursued through exploitation of land and labor. Settler colonialism and anti-Black racial domination are the foundation for United States capitalism because they focus on accumulation by exploitation and oppression. This oppression is not a historical event but actually a system that lays the foundation and conditions for capitalism/neoliberalism to facilitate evolved forms of settler colonialism like gentrification.

Most importantly, land is the sacred regenerative ground that connects us to our ancestors, the home of our nonhuman kinfolk, our food and pharmacy, our library, and the source of all that sustains us. This understanding is an important paradigm shift; Indigenous peoples around the world have not surrendered the meaning of and relationship to land despite colonization. This idea of *grounded normativity*, originated by Glen Coulthard, is the idea that the purpose of land is cultural and reciprocal to humans and nonhumans alike, as opposed to being commercial and commodifiable.

This unique understanding of land and its stewardship presents some complications when we explore the return of land. In the settler colonial context, returning land is about transferring ownership. In the United States, we have an example of an alleged land transfer in a settler colonial context. In 1851, the United States enacted the Indian Appropriations Act, which relegated Native American tribes onto semi-sovereign land called reservations. Though the United States positioned the migration as voluntary, it was coerced by all accounts.

When I was six years old, my family took a trip to Arizona to see the Grand Canyon and to learn more about Native American heritage. Even at that young age, I knew America first belonged to the Native Americans. As we drove from our home in the Mojave Desert to Dine land, down Interstate 10 in our old air conditioner–less sedan, I was in awe of the copper-colored landscapes and painted sunsets. I felt a visceral familiarity with the extreme temperatures, dry heat, tumbleweeds, and trailer homes. However, I was shocked to witness the inhumane realities of life on the "rez." As we drove by communities, I saw children with flies on their faces outside playing with recycled cans, mothers selling turquoise jewelry for tourists while sitting on crushed velvet fabric, and a few men riding on the cargo beds of pickup trucks from trailer home to trailer home, all in one-hundred-degree heat.

Many years later, I learned the inconsistent tourist economy was the main source of income for the people living on Indigenous land, and that was by design. The American federal government owned and managed almost all matters of economic development on reservations. This "return of (some) land" to Native Americans in the form of reservations was both woefully insufficient and an insult to the Native Americans given the sheer enormity of the theft and violence that had been inflicted on them. The US government designed reservations to (re)produce poverty by unilaterally situating them in areas away from population centers, fertile land, and other vital resources.

By design, poverty and dehumanization are not limited to life on reservations. One of my first memories, and fights, happened in kindergarten when a white child called me "a nigger from Africa," making specific reference to the Save the Children TV commercial, a popular fundraising commercial for starving East African children in the mid-1990s. From a young age, I understood I was Black and that was beautiful. I did not know what *nigger* meant, and frankly, that is not what upset me at the time. What upset me was the disrespect, deception, and delusion I felt because a white child had the audacity to make me feel like I didn't belong at that Episcopalian Christian elementary school because I might be poor and hungry. The Save the Children commercial made trauma porn out of one of the worst humanitarian events in recent history, the Ethiopian famine. Children who looked like me were reduced to being undesirable, poor, and uncivilized, with flies on their faces and distended bellies.

I was reminded of this insult on my first trip to that Native American reservation. That day, when my family stopped for a snack, I was hotter than the fresh greasy fry bread in my hands and I was enraged. Though I couldn't articulate this at the time, I experienced a kind of spiritual connection with the Native American kids. This community looked a lot like the streets of Bole, Addis Ababa—but this wasn't "underdeveloped" Africa; this was America, hours away from where I lived. I began to search for connections. Maybe the land is one of the few things left to connect Native American children to their ancestors, heritage, and culture, like the land of Ethiopia to my family? Maybe those children are experiencing hunger by design of government neglect and divestment, like my cousins in Ethiopia? Maybe those children were harassed by white children, like I was? Maybe we are interconnected?

Awareness and naming of a spiritual and metaphysical connection to others is something we can all access, and it is not limited to other humans. When we remember and reckon with the depth of destruction and theft, it allows us to facilitate the material return of stewardship and protection of sacred ground, which must include Indigenous understandings and relationships to land to protect Earth for generations to come.

A reconciliation process can only occur after settlers return stewardship of occupied land to Indigenous and African peoples. All of us came from the Earth and our survival depends on understanding and connecting to the land. Settler colonialism, by design, disrupts and destroys our relationships with animals, water, and our food sources. Land return demands food and land sovereignty, and the philosophical and political approach to living free of settler influences.

LANGUAGE

The bullet was the means of the physical subjugation.
Language was the means of the spiritual subjugation.
—NGŨGĨ WA THIONG'O, *Decolonising the Mind*

Kenyan novelist and decolonial thinker Ngũgĩ wa Thiong'o, formerly James Ngugi, was heavily influenced by West Indian political scientist and psychologist Frantz Fanon. In Fanon's book *Black Skin, White Masks* he explained that the colonial project is holistic and comprehensive; it does not leave any aspect of our reality or personhood untouched. Thiong'o highlights the subtle and subversive metaphysical empire, distinct from the physical empire, as being what causes mental dislocation and disorientation that often goes unnoticed. Everything is informed by colonization, from our names to the syntax with which we choose to communicate.

Thiong'o's book *Decolonising the Mind* presented a devastating revelation for me that required me to reflect and question my reality. I am a first-generation Ethiopian. I was born and raised in the United States by parents who, against the odds, arrived and married in the US. In our home, my parents maintained the language, rituals, and customs of Ethiopia, even when the US was inhospitable. Despite having conversational proficiency in my mother tongue, Amharic, I still struggle to access the poetic and metaphorical elements of the language. All my dreams, visions, and thoughts have been uttered and understood in English, the colonizers' language. Mastering my mother tongue would grant me connection to generations of ancestors who used this language to fight and defeat invaders, and I could understand the wordplay and playful humor as relayed by Ethiopian *azmaris*. In Amharic, and many other African languages, the function of language is not just to communicate, but to appreciate and honor the suggestive, magical power of language. Whether it is reinforced by wordplay, riddles, harmony, allegories, proverbs, transpositions of syllables, or through non-sensical but musically arranged words, the language of our heritage is the vehicle for our culture.

Our mother tongue enhanced our imagination; through colorful arrangements of images and symbols, we created a unique worldview.

Thiong'o describes the territory of the imagination and the mind as the "third empire." This is where settler colonization lays the "cultural bomb." In *Decolonising the Mind* he prophetically said:

> The effect of the cultural bomb is to annihilate a people's belief in their names, in their languages, in their environment, in their heritage of struggle, in their unity, in their capacities and ultimately in themselves. It makes them see their past as one wasteland of non-achievement

and it makes them want to distance themselves from that wasteland. It makes them want to identify with that which is furthest removed from themselves, for instance, with other peoples' languages rather than their own. It makes them identify with that which is decadent and reactionary, all those forces that would stop their own springs of life. It even plants serious doubts about the moral righteousness of struggle. Possibilities of triumph or victory are seen as remote, ridiculous dreams. The intended results are despair, despondency and a collective death-wish.

One vehicle for coerced assimilation, cultural annihilation, and the collective death-wish in North America was the residential school. Residential schools were abusive, and in some cases deadly, boarding schools for Native American and First Nation children. Some Indigenous parents were misled by the United States government to believe that sending their children to these schools would help Native nations create English-speaking liaisons to improve relations with the United States. Other families experienced having their children forcibly removed. In both cases, children's souls and their physical and spiritual beings were tortured and murdered.

Upon arrival at these schools, the children had their hair cut so they would abandon their traditional long hairstyles and appear more Eurocentric. In Indigenous and African cultures, growing and braiding hair is a sacred ritual; people only tend to cut their hair when someone in their community transitions, becoming an ancestor. As a result, the residential schools were regularly filled with children wailing because they understood having their hair cut to mean someone at home was dying.

And the trauma did not end there. Once in a classroom, students were exclusively taught Eurocentric/white superiority doctrine in English. In addition, they labored in the fields for most of the day, were harshly punished, were forced to maintain militaristic schedules, and were kept malnourished. At many residential school sites, school administrators built makeshift cemeteries to accommodate the high rate of child deaths. This, however, should come as no surprise since one of the first residential schools was founded by United States General Richard Henry Pratt under the motto "Kill the Indian in him and save the man"; Pratt went on to say "the only good Indian is a dead one." With this prevailing sentiment guiding the pedagogy and purpose of residential schools, it is clear they were a death-making institution by design.

Residential schools and African missionary schools had a few things in common. In Africa, Christian missionary boarding schools were popular colonial mechanisms meant to erase and eliminate the language, culture, and spirituality of Indigenous Africans and to coerce assimilation. Like residential schools, they were also prisonesque and lacked humane living conditions. They had no clean water, they were overcrowded, and the children were not safe from rampant sexual and physical violence. Some families refused to assimilate and resisted domination, but these actions often resulted in violence that compromised the safety and generational survival of a community. These carceral schools were designed to erase and eliminate the language and culture of the children settlers saw as racially inferior. These schools operated as an extension of the settler colonial project to subjugate, physically and spiritually, some of the most vulnerable people in society, children.

This settler colonial pattern of separating children from families is one that continues today in the United States child welfare systems and at borders with immigrants.

Colonization intentionally, subconsciously, and violently invades and operates in our mental models. The impact of colonization reaches far beyond its effect of robbing us of our linguistic heritage and inheritance and extends into the spirit world and the ways we understand ourselves and the world around us. In many Native and First Nation communities, people who are gifted with two or more spirits—female, male, and/or intersex—are known as *Two-Spirit*. This way of understanding gender identity is not binary, and this self-identified third gender term communicates many important community roles. Two-Spirits are endowed with spiritual sanction and supernatural visions, and as a result, they have specialized roles in contributing to the community, often becoming chiefs, healers, and weavers. Settlers disrupted, denied, and destroyed identities and concepts like Two-Spirit, which resulted in loss of identity, traditions, and, in many cases, life.

The occupation and colonization of our mind and the way we think appears in the way we communicate who we are and who we can be. The lifegiving work of liberating colonized and oppressed peoples out of the English (or other colonial languages) metaphysical empire and neocolonialism is optimally done in our mother tongues and traditions. In lieu of that, it is important that radical and revolutionary literature, this text included, is written in a way that is both easily understood by and resonates with the spirit of oppressed peoples and that it connects with their past experiences and present self-identification.

LIFESTYLE

They want our rhythm but not our blues.
—BLACK PROVERB

During the eighteenth and nineteenth centuries, Europe engaged in unfathomable theft and destruction of land, people, languages, and resources, but the theft did not end there; colonizers stole precious art, artifacts, and other cultural treasures from Africa to decorate their houses and museums. Strangely, while enjoying the cultural experiences and treasures of colonized people, the settlers render all that is traditional, ancestral, African, and Indigenous primitive and obsolete. Today, colonial theft and erasure continues with the stealing and exploitation of Black, African, and Indigenous cultures, talents, and genius to enrich the lifestyle of the powerful.

In the United States, rock and roll, a genre of music inspired and pioneered by Sister Rosetta Tharpe, a queer Black woman from Arkansas, has largely been misattributed to white men. Raised in the Black gospel music tradition, Sister Rosetta Tharpe brought her spiritual tradition, personality, and whole self to her songs and performances. When we listen to music created by Black people, particularly Black queer women, we hear a miracle of sound—not just the inspiration and improvisation that Black artists bring to music, but the spirit of those who've struggled against enslavement, settler colonialism, anti-Blackness, homophobia, and misogynoir.

Despite the ongoing proliferation of Black music and culture around the world, loving Black music and culture has not meant loving Black people. So how did this genre, rooted in Black traditions and people, become understood as belonging to white people? Through *white male hegemony*, the pattern and belief that white males are the authority and cultural ideal. In *Everything but the Burden: What White People Are Taking from Black Culture*, Greg Tate, writer, critic, and producer, curates a series of essays to exhaustively demonstrate how white people rob Black people of their culture but deliberately leave the burdens and stresses of anti-Blackness, poverty, and exploitation. In other words, white people see Black people as objects for their entertainment, not as humans. Moreover, this kind of white-on-Black cultural theft results in the denial and diminishment of the talent, innovation, and genius of Black artists and is often coupled with literal theft in predatory economic terms. From exploitative record deals to wholesale theft of intellectual labor without acknowledgment, this violent erasure is reframed and rebranded as "sharing" and "learning from other cultures." This is an age-old tactic of rebranding and reframing to gaslight those who are victims of the ongoing settler colonial project.

Settler colonialism does not stop there. It continues to transform the way of life and hinder the ability to deliver new life to the oppressed.

American gynecology has its origins in the exploitation of and experimentation on enslaved Black women. In 1844, James Marion Sims, "the father of modern gynecology," famously performed experiments on enslaved women who he leased to other doctors for continued experimentation. Most often these experiments were performed without any form of anesthesia. Thus the Black woman's experience with Western healthcare is defined by subjectivity and invisibility. This pattern extends to today, with the continued gendered violence Black women experience in healthcare where their humanity is erased or denied.

The settler way of life literally and figuratively disabled people, changing their physical and psychological worlds. A recent example of the impairments that result from settler colonialism was the discovery that the Israeli government was operating state mandates for contraception of Ethiopian Jews disproportionately and without consent. These actions amount to depressed fertility at best, or forced sterilization and genocide at worst. Similarly, in 2012, in my home state of California, the prison system forced sterilizations without adequate consent of Black and brown inmates; this was a kind of racist, sexist eugenics effort to "to curb the population of unwanted individuals or people with disabilities" as state assemblywoman Wendy Carrillo observed in the *Guardian* article "Survivors of California's Forced Sterilizations." California prisons sterilized thousands of people because the state deemed they were criminal, feeble-minded, or deviant. This ironic settler labeling and theft of dignity and choice amounts to colonial reproductive violence that threatens the safety, bodily sovereignty, and integrity of women and gender-nonconforming people.

Psychologically and philosophically, colonialism has left a lasting imprint on how Black people view ourselves and our bodies that continues today. In the settler colonial context, disability is understood as an impairment that people possess that disallows them from fully participating in society. This definition coupled with settler logic of normative development creates limiting binaries of lived experiences and disrupts the development of identity, self-determination, and community membership.

According to many Native American communities, children are gifts from the Sky World to the entire community and must be cherished and protected. When a child presents as disabled, their inherent nature of being a gift remains, and the community understands that the child has experiences that will make the community better. Many Indigenous traditions and disabled activists contend that disability is a social condition not a social identity. As Kim E. Nielsen, a disability scholar, notes in *A Disability History of the United States*, Native American conceptions of disability are unique. They have no language equivalent or even translatable concept for the word *disabled*; the closest translatable phrase is simply "being different." Wellness in Native American and many African cultures is defined as a "wholeness of existence"—that every aspect of an individual's reality is interconnected and interwoven with nature, community, the spirits, and the elements. The stark binary of "normal" and "abnormal" that dominates settler colonial culture does not exist. Our identity—who we are and how we understand ourselves and others—has been poisoned by colonial categorizations. This colonial logic extends beyond disability to gender and all other facets of our identity.

The lifestyle and ways of being in the settler colonial context is not limited to countries directly colonized. I was raised in an Ethiopian household where Amharic was primarily spoken, and we often discussed the history of our motherland and its hard-fought resistance to Italian colonization. Though Ethiopia was never colonized, many Ethiopians—my parents included, learned and embodied the physical, psychological, and spiritual violence brought by occupying Italians. My paternal grandfather fought the Italian occupation and was kept in a concentration camp at the border of Somaliland for more than five years. There he was exposed to varied colonial tactics of torture and terror. Though he was released, that violent experience stayed with him and was passed on to following generations. For example, my grandfather was not able to maintain a healthy and loving relationship with my grandmother, so he raised my father, his first-born son, alone with what our family calls "discipline," but with what amounts to cruel and unusual punishment, much like the torture he experienced in the internment camp. This style of child rearing continued until my father was thirteen when his father died of liver disease. When my father started his own family twenty years later, he continued to affirm the intergenerational inheritance of Ethiopian defiance and decolonization but did not interrogate his albeit limited exposure to colonization and his reproduction of its harms.

As a young, first-generation, immigrant Black girl born into this context, I struggled a great deal. I was caught between experiencing Ethiopian patriarchal traditions at home, along with unresolved intergenerational trauma, and living in a country that rejected all parts of me. Despite the rejection, I found ways to love myself, one of which was taking great care of my hair. From Tigray to box braids to press and curls, I explored and cultivated my crown. African and Black Americans use our hair and its many styles as ways to convey who we are, from tribal affiliation and marital status to how we are feeling on a particular day. Hair has been a way for Black girls and women to share our identity and communicate with others. Like many Black girls, I generated great pride in the cultivation and care of my hair and the many styles and ways my curls transformed.

This practice of tending to my hair continued into high school, coinciding with my high school rebelliousness. One day during my freshman year, my father caught me wearing makeup to school, a forbidden activity. In a complete rage because of my disobedience, my father grabbed office scissors and cut twenty inches of my recently pressed hair. I was in complete shock—all the years of tending and growing my hair, the connection my hair gave me to other Black girls, and the sacred and spiritual relationship I had built around its care were all taken away in one moment. Much like the children in residential schools, I was subjected to the cruel, traumatizing, and dehumanizing experience of my hair being cut. My father's internalized trauma and colonial logic of extreme and unusual punishment, without regard for my adolescence or humanity, is a reminder of how colonization has penetrated all aspects of our lifestyles, even for people who were never formally under colonial rule.

Our lifestyles are punctuated by our rituals, routines, norms, values, ceremonies, and other formal and informal expressions. They hold special sanctity and significance to our sense of self and worldmaking efforts. How we live our lives give us dignity, but most importantly, our ways of being create strong families, neighborhoods, and communities. The work of cultivating kinship with other people, nature, and the world around us is, in my opinion, the most important work of creation.

THE FOURTH L: LABOR

So much of the land, language, and lifestyle we experience is often designed for capitalistic purposes, for commodification and consumption. Outside of our homes, most people spend their days laboring. Whether in an office or on a factory floor, our workplace is an extension of settler values both in the formal, built environment and in the informal day-to-day practices. So much of what workers do and how they do it, and even the spaces they work in, is designed as an extension of slavery. The enslavement of kidnapped Africans inspired (and continues to inspire) modern business management, and relatedly, a variety of design practices.

In an article titled "How Slavery Inspired Modern Business Management" in *Boston Review*, Caitlin Rosenthal discusses how Scudder Klyce, a nineteenth-century naval officer and outspoken proponent of business management science, argued that scientific management is a system that "consists of the able person's taking the lead in giving 'orders' in the cases where he is of superior ability, and the others' submitting: it is the relationship of master and slave, regardless of how otherwise it may be named." From the manager's perspective, control and measurement were the essential characteristics of scientific management. Obviously, the obsession with power and precision is significantly different from the "whip and a watch" used on enslaved peoples on plantations—but the spirit of work is a pattern that continues today.

The most striking parallel between slavery and scientific management is seen in the *task system*, one of the most important ideas in business today. Henry Laurence Gantt, who is commonly associated with creating the Gantt chart, though he did not design it, was responsible for task system proliferation. The Gantt chart is a scheduling tool that has its roots in slavery. The seemingly innocuous chart and its associated task system originated as a way to organize enslaved labor under slavery. Gantt's goal was never to abolish this original slavery-based system but to adapt it to modern needs. In Caitlin Rosenthal's *Accounting for Slavery: Masters and Management* she describes the explicit replication of slavery's extractive techniques:

> Under the task system, an enslaved person would be assigned a set "task" or quota that he or she was expected to complete by the end of the day; this was in contrast to the gang system, where enslaved people labored under constant supervision for a set period of time. In some cases, slavers who used the task system even gave monetary bonuses for achievement above set targets. They "dangled the carrot" in a way that resembles not just Gantt's methods but those of the gig economy today. Indeed, except for the base payment and the critically important ability for workers to quit, Gantt's new system was in nearly every respect the same as the system used by some slaveholders, a fact that Gantt made no attempt to hide. Rather, he acknowledged that the

word "task" was "disliked by many men" because of its connection to slavery, and he regarded this negative connotation as its "principal disadvantage."

The enslavement of Black people in America shows us how one arrangement of control, precision, and "maximizing efficiencies" can evolve to become an extremely sophisticated exploitation that produces a horrifying toll. We see this pattern continue today as workers fight inhumane working conditions that employ these tactics. Workers at factories like those of Amazon and Frito-Lay have been fighting unsafe work conditions, wage theft, and the extreme monitoring of tasks that have produced a nonstop work environment with no bathroom breaks, paid sick leave, or living wages.

Harvard Business Review (*HBR*) often highlights ideas and offers guidelines managers can follow to lead their organization and the broader economy. In 2012, in its ninetieth anniversary issue, the magazine featured several essays from Frederick Winslow Taylor, the pioneer of management sciences and an outspoken champion of slavery-based tactics in the workplace. Later in 2019, *HBR* published "The Right Way to Lead Design Thinking," an essay to guide leaders to more efficient project management. Aside from the article's distressing title that implies that there is one objective and universal way to lead design thinking, this piece goes on to promote that "even more than other change-management processes, design thinking requires active and effective leadership to keep efforts on a path to success." This logic of "effective leadership" for a "path of success" is reminiscent of a master overseeing tasks to ensure profit. This way of thinking about labor is an extension of the evolution of business management's approach predicated on control, efficiency, and effectiveness and its use of its philosophical underpinnings of manipulation and exploitation.

The heritage of doing business in this way, in the United States and Europe, includes tandem, deeply intertwined experiences of innovation and extreme violence. This was especially true on the plantation and is still true, in many ways, for scientific management and design thinking business practices. In this way, traditional business practices and scale innovation are byproducts of bondage. Reckoning with the denial and discomfort of our past can help us more clearly see the deep connections between colonization, capitalism, control, and creation.

HISTORY, AS TOLD BY THE HOSTAGES

Until lions have their historians, tales of the hunt shall always glorify the hunters.
—AFRICAN PROVERB

What gets remembered is a function of who's doing the remembering.
—BETTY REID SOSKIN, American national park ranger

In the settler context, the events of the past are regarded as "history." The word *history* originates from the Greek word *historia*, which means the act of seeking knowledge. It is commonly understood to be an objective, linear reflection of past events. Recorded history has been regarded largely as a trusted source of unbiased and factual information on past events. However, history as told by white and European people has distorted, denied, and absolved the atrocities and barbarism they manifested and exacted. It focuses on *androcentric scientific knowledge*—in other words, centering male heterosexual views of objectivity and universality that are not "polluted" by lived experience. This kind of recollection does not recall the past but instead a colonial delusion, one that asserts complete objectivity and universality by virtue of its authority and might. Like many concepts exploited by settler colonization and capitalism, history has new meaning. The irony here is how severely it contrasts with the initial intent of the word.

Neocolonialism, led by the US, has offered exploited and oppressed peoples a pattern of pathological amnesia and a commitment to denial of lived experience, evidence, and facts. Around the world, we've been hoodwinked to believe colonization is a righteous endeavor of the discovery of new lands, the conquest of barbaric peoples, and the civilization of "new" worlds. This long-held perspective is far from the reality, but that doesn't stop it from continuing to proliferate. The hunters, the many former and current colonial powers, romanticize their former empires and territories. Prevailing cultural sentiments and formal documents in those colonizing countries still, in many ways, convey the belief that colonial powers improved underdeveloped and uncivilized territories. In the not-so-distant past, elementary schools like the one I attended taught history from textbooks that very briefly, in three pages to be precise, described the four hundred years of kidnapping and enslaving of Africans in the Transatlantic slave trade as a kind of worker arrangement intended to help civilize and Christianize Black people. There was no mention of the cruel and brutal conditions of enslavement, or the sociopathic behaviors of slaveholders, or the connection to the obvious pattern of violence and extraction first exacted on the Native Americans as the white settlers occupied and stole Native land. Most importantly, the history of slave revolts, marooning, and other resistance efforts are auspiciously omitted in textbooks.

This version of history doubles down on distortion and denial in an effort to absolve settlers' responsibility for enslavement and to create an identity of settler colonial superiority. In other words, the American and Eurocentric education systems manifest and deliver the values of settler colonial context subtly from an early age. Having read this version of history and attended a school that allowed this dehumanizing and grossly inaccurate version to be taught, I am concerned not just for me and my peers but for the generations to come. As a Black parent, I believe that it seems foolish and dangerous to trust an education system designed by white, land-owning, Christian men that allows them to tell their versions of history. Whether intentionally or not, the writers and teachers of these texts promote erasure and dehumanization while simultaneously diminishing the heritage and self-confidence of Black and Indigenous people.

It is important to note that the history of enslavement and genocide should not be considered Black or Indigenous history but rather white history, as it is the violent, horrific, and shameful past of white settlers. The refusal to uncover and give voice to colonization's unsavory past continues today in the US as efforts to incorporate critical race theory in schools are met with intense resistance and refusal from primarily white Americans. History, as relayed by colonizers, can never capture the full humanity of those it oppresses or the full nature of the brutal subjugation and spiritual assault on African and Indigenous peoples. The settlers' history cannot grasp the onslaught of everyday violence and psychological harm passively inflicted. Settler colonial accounts of history deny the land, language, and lifestyle—in other words, the humanity and existence—of the oppressed. History told by the colonizers is, by design, made to diminish and dehumanize—all under the guise of objectivity.

Western society and settler colonial powers regard maps, a seemingly objective representation of land and sea, as tools to navigate from place to place. Many people regard maps and navigation technology as practical and useful. The Mercator map, created in 1569, was originally used as a cylindrical projection for colonial navigation. This map is not drawn to scale by design; it represents Europe and North America as inaccurately large and continents like Africa and South America as shrunken in an effort to consciously and subconsciously diminish colonized countries and exaggerate colonial powers. African and other Indigenous people are keenly aware that maps are tools for colonialism and exploitation. Maps visually memorialize the location of grand scale theft, enslavement, subjugation, and the traumatic rupture caused by colonial violence. Maps created by colonizers are artifacts designed to designate property (both people and places) and impose subtle normalization of the logic of colonization's existence.

Colonial maps represent a way of life that enforces settler borders, control mechanisms, and barriers to movement. Whether the walls of prisons or the borders between states, borders are separations that have resounding implications for the oppressed. During the time of enslavement, borders were the legal demarcations between slave plantations and the wilderness, or the Ohio River and "free" territory beyond it. Borders are also societal and maintain your status or position. To be Black, around the world, means to be outside the border of humanity. The way individuals and institutions have been able to arbitrarily enslave, imprison, kill, or otherwise harm Black people for centuries is evidence of Black people existing outside the boundary of humanity. In literal and figurative terms, maps violently displace and erase relationships and create borders that disrupt communities, identities, and sacred memories that are inherently connected to the land in material, emotional, and spiritual ways.

Therefore, I submit that we reconsider the intention and impact of recorded history. It's not enough to critically examine the past; we must explore alternative ways of learning, knowing, and being that don't cause casual and cascading violence. Let's stop valorizing settler ways of meaning making and question the very notion of history in its current form and its role in facilitating past and present erasure, extraction, and exploitation. Let's abandon the preference for objectivity and engage with decolonial Black feminist knowledge production, which tells us that all knowledge comes from lived experience, relationship, and subjectivity. To be explicit, this also means valuing and validating knowledge that is created outside of the academy or corporate settings.

Decolonial Black feminist methodology invites us to be self-critical and to come to terms with our relative privilege and positionality. In doing so, we create the possibility of producing our own knowledge and ways of being. By offering compelling alternatives, African and Indigenous ways of knowing and recalling the past pose a threat to the status quo. Lakota medicine man John Fire Lame Deer describes the powerful and sardonic contrast between his world and the world of "the white man" in his book *Lame Deer, Seeker of Visions*:

> Before our white brothers came to civilize us we had no jails. Therefore, we had no criminals. You can't have criminals without a jail. We had no locks or keys, and so we had no thieves. If a man was so poor that he had no horse, tipi or blanket, someone gave him these things. We were too uncivilized to set much value on personal belongings. We wanted to have things only in order to give them away. We had no money, and therefore a man's worth couldn't be measured by it. We had no written law, no attorneys or politicians, therefore we couldn't cheat. We really were in a bad way before the white men came, and I

don't know how we managed to get along without these basic things which, we are told, are absolutely necessary to make a civilized society.

Ultimately, this process of exploring alternative ways of understanding the past will help us give "language, names, and faces" to the "unnamed baby" we inherited, as poet lucille clifton invites us to do in her poem "i am accused of tending to the past," and enable us to go get what we forgot so that we can move forward.

You may be wondering why it is necessary to explore so much suffering and oppression as we re-member. It is, of course, because the acquisition of deep justice cannot be delivered without it. The deliberate displacement and erasure of African Indigenous languages, lands, and lifestyles require a kind of cognitive justice that allows us to understand the world in more ways than one so that we can begin the re-membering process.

(Re)Memory: Fiction, Folklore, or Fact

Truth passes through fire and does not burn.
—AFRICAN PROVERB

Memory, the power of recalling what has been learned over time, is a practice that is passed through generations. Memory is a way to understand the past that includes oral traditions and personal narratives that ultimately shape our collective consciousness. Most importantly, memory affirms the humanity of the oppressed by embodying our struggle, in spite of colonial rape, violence, theft, and exploitation, and it is the self-acknowledgment of what is not presentable under the Western rules of knowledge. Many Indigenous African practices assert that objects, organisms (including humans), and organizations have collective memory and contexts. To deny this lived experience is to deny their existence. These traditions also know that knowledge and meaning are co-created and community owned, with elders being a kind of library of this rich Indigenous knowledge.

Black feminist writer bell hooks connects our Indigenous memory to the decolonial struggle in her book *Black Looks*:

As red and black people decolonize our minds we cease to place value solely on the written document. We give ourselves back memory. We acknowledge that the ancestors speak to us in a place beyond written history.

Womanist thinker and writer Alice Walker uses fiction to create awareness of subjugated knowledges specifically to connect the ties between Native and Black people in America. In her novel, *The Temple of My Familiar*, a Black woman character is asked why she loves Native Americans, and she responds,

> They open doors inside me. It's as if they're keys. To rooms inside myself. I find a door inside and it's as if I hear a humming from behind it, and then I get inside somehow, with the key the old ones give me, and as I stumble about in the darkness of the room, I begin to feel the stirring in myself, the humming of the room, and my heart starts to expand with the absolute feeling of bravery, or love, or audacity, or commitment. It becomes a light, and that light enters me, by osmosis, and a part of me that was not clear before is clarified.

Black feminist fiction writers like Walker evoke a process of re-membering that is essential for the political self-recovery of colonized and oppressed peoples. *Rememory*, a concept created by historical fiction writer Toni Morrison, is the practice of recollecting and remembering, as in reassembling the members of the body, the family, the population of the past. Returning to the memories becomes a ritual or a place we visit regularly, a place that helps us recall that which we forgot we knew. Morrison coined the concept in her novel *Beloved*. The main character is a woman named Sethe who was formerly enslaved. She was able to recall fragmented memories and connect to Africa from where her ancestors were kidnapped. In her rememory, Sethe realizes that the fate of enslaved Black people is to be forgotten and erased, like cattle, never recorded or remembered.

> Some things you forget. Other things you never do. But it's not. Places, places are still there. If a house burns down, it's gone, but the place—the picture of it—stays, and not just in my rememory, but out there, in the world. What I remember is a picture floating around out there outside my head. I mean, even if I don't think it, even if I die,

the picture of what I did, or knew, or saw is still out there. Right in the place where it happened.

Sethe's reply is in rememory, or in her own words, "remembering something she had forgotten she knew." White slaveholders can claim her body, her milk, her labor, but not her memory. Rememory, like memories, is often connected to trauma or a unique experience. The rememory is excavated through the people who shared their memories, written or orally, with others. It is a combination of past and present, and a stark contrast to linear versions of Western history. Some might argue that it is unreliable to rely on extremely traumatic or difficult memories because they are sometimes distorted, disregarded, mutable, excluded, or dissociated from our recollections. That is true. That said, how reliable are the delusions and distortions of history as told by the settlers?

Who decides and arbitrates what is true or fact? Is there an objective truth? Can there be multiple truths?

Decolonial feminist scholar Jeong-eun Rhee is a Korean migrant American educational qualitative researcher who has studied and attempted new ways to explore, notice, feel, know, and experience rememory across time, geography, languages, and ways of knowing and being. Through poetry, fiction, and theories, she employs a different way of learning and understanding rememory as a collective and intergenerational meaning-making experience. Her book *Decolonial Feminist Research: Haunting, Rememory, and Mothers* set out to employ rememory specifically as a path for exploring, imagining, and engendering healing and wholeness. She suggested the knowledge embodied in Black, African, and Indigenous peoples is relevant, useful, appropriate, and legitimate, even within the settler colonial Western science regime.

The past pattern of history as told by settlers is meant to enforce binaries and neglect and reject the traumas and memories of those who are incarcerated, disabled, gender nonconforming, or female, as well as the destitute and other exploited peoples. Questioning and searching for the relationship between the past, memories, and trauma is important in the excavation effort to remember. Rememory is one of many promising ways to consider and recall the past, but it is not the only way.

Colonial Visitations: History, Horror, and Hauntings

We need to know where we live in order to imagine living elsewhere.
We need to imagine living elsewhere before we can live there.
      —AVERY GORDON, *Ghostly Matters:*
         Haunting and the Sociological Imagination

Ghosts arrive when there is unfinished business. They hold the brutal secrets of the past and forebode a future reckoning. Selena Wilson, activist, nonprofit leader, and my long-time sister in struggle, often shares that at a very young age, growing up in East Oakland, California, she saw ghosts. Ghosts of her friends, classmates, and neighbors murdered at the hands of the state, and ghosts of the thriving village of elders who were incarcerated for nonviolent drug offenses. These ghosts continue to remind her of what was violently stolen from her and her community.

Erasure of knowledge, history, and ways of living lays bare the structural and violent exploitation of peoples and lands, the consequences of settler colonialism.

History as we know it is haunted, a place where ghosts appear and reappear. In the Ethiopian tradition, and many other African traditions, hauntings are untold stories of historical violence, and they exist to expose the horrific legacies of the past. Hauntings are the consistent reappearances of ghosts and they are unavoidable. The stories of ghosts and hauntings as described by sociologist Avery Gordon explore the hidden passageways, not only of the individual psyche, but also of a community's historical consciousness.

Globally, anti-Blackness is a haunting, one designed to reproduce settler colonial power relations and racism. In the process of recovering history, hauntings demonstrate how reconstructing history is essentially an imaginative act. Centrally concerned with the issues of communal memory, cultural transmission, and group inheritance, stories of "haunting" share the plot device and master metaphor of the ghost as a go-between, an enigmatic transitional figure moving between past and present, death and life, one culture and another. In other words, hauntings represent a return to the supernatural for direction.

In *Ghostly Matters*, Gordon writes about societal ghosts and the ideas of complex relationships and complex personhood. She contends that nothing in society is as simple as the titles given to it and that societal ghosts frame our ways of thinking and acting. Given that history has been written and affirmed by the powerful, we must concern ourselves with the nature of power—the force present in every interaction. Gordon recalls Toni Morrison's *The Bluest Eye* and borrows the concept of "furniture without memories" to make clear the omnipresence of power:

> Furniture without memories can be imagined as power structures whose existence we navigate daily without questioning it. The chair we sit in, that shapes our posture, whose structure guides what we see and how comfortable we feel.

She extends this metaphor to a sunken couch:

> that sad and sunken couch that sags in just that place where an unrememberable past and an unimaginable future force us to sit day after day and the conceptual abstractions because everything of significance happens there among the inert furniture and the monumental social architecture.

We accept, without question, the structures and rituals, like inert furniture, that shape our behaviors but are so ingrained that we do not ask for their past or purpose. Why is the cushion sunken? Because it's always been that way. Why do we sit on the sunken cushion on the couch? Because we always have.

To explore the past and present settler colonial conditions, we must question the ubiquitous and mundane, take heed to hauntings, and act, but most importantly, we must invite alternatives to reconstruct a history that acknowledges our collective sacred and complex personhood.

Ethnographic Refusal

> *Indians have been cursed above all other people in history. Indians have anthropologists.*
>
> —VINE DELORIA JR., author, theologian, historian, and activist; from *Custer Died for Your Sins: An Indian Manifesto*

One of the first steps in the traditional design process, during the inquiry phase, is ethnographic research. *Ethnography* has its roots in anthropology as a common research method utilized to observe issues, peoples, relationships, and cultures. It is a means of knowledge accumulation and production and it has been critical in keeping the settler colonial project operating. *Anthropology*, as an academic field, evolved from nineteenth century sociology in Europe and focused on small cultural groups in Africa, Asia, and the Americas. Strangely, anthropology has imagined itself to be a voice, and in some disciplinary iterations, the voice of the colonized. For many anthropologists, ethnography is a way Indigenous people have been known and sometimes are still known.

Anthropologist Audra Simpson, a Kahnawake academic, coined the concept *ethnographic refusal*, which describes how Indigenous people are actively shaping how information about Indigenous culture and experiences is made available. Simpson draws from her personal experiences conducting traditional ethnographic research in her home community to describe how research participants avoid discussing topics that they do not want known or misrepresented by outsiders—particularly academics.

In a contribution entitled "R-Words: Refusing Research," Indigenous scholars Eve Tuck and K. Wayne Yang suggest that all refusals are generative because they redirect the focus of research toward processes of power and wealth, thus decentering narratives of damage or destruction. Doing this sets limits to what issues are known by, and therefore responded to through, a logic of settler colonialism.

Ethnography, a discipline born of the context of colonialism, is not just voyeuristic, it is inherently exploitative and an expression of settler values. Let's explore the widely cited and popular Maslow Hierarchy of Needs. Abraham Maslow, a white American psychologist, is credited with creating a framework to classify the needs of the people he studied, starting with their physiological needs and culminating in an apex of self-actualization. This model was a product of weeks spent living with the Siksika, also known as the Blackfoot Reserve. The Blackfoot lifestyle offers an alternative way of thinking that considers and incorporates the whole community. It goes beyond Maslow's framework to conclude in self-actualization and continues to society, nation, and generational legacy to create cultural perpetuity. Despite Maslow's gross appropriation and theft of the Siksika way of life, the model is still predicated on settler epistemology of individualism. The denial of the influence of Indigenous worldview coupled with the distortion of Indigenous values is one of the many ways ethnography erases and exploits.

In the *Scientific American* article "Anthropology Association Apologizes to Native Americans for the Field's Legacy of Harm," Vernon Finley, the chairman of the Confederated Salish and Kootenai Tribes, reflected on his childhood and shared that the "onslaught of anthropologists" who came to his tribe to "record" the elders' stories almost always interpreted them inaccurately.

More importantly, tribal elders were not told what the "experts" planned to do with the information. This approach of leaving the "user" out, often used in design, is not only harmful but leads to incorrect inquiry and implementation. The long-standing harm and damage of anthropologists most often began with good intentions. But good intentions don't address or resolve the harm inflicted; in fact, as my elders say, the road to hell is paved with good intentions. Here in the US, at the end of 2022, the American Anthropological Association issued an apology to Indigenous communities to acknowledge and address their role in extraction and exploitation.

While this is a starting point from which anthropologists can begin the reckoning and potentially the reconciliation process, those who have committed harm must move beyond words, even beyond mechanical actions, to the very difficult work of behavior change.

I've worked as a community organizer on many campaigns—from the Justice for Janitors campaign in Los Angeles, to the first living wage campaign in the United States, to a homecare worker strike campaign in Millbrae, California, to political campaigns for President Obama, to the founding of the Parent Innovation Institute in Oakland. Through it all I've learned that addressing and acknowledging the past, as well as the current conditions, and thereby earning trust and building power with oppressed people, has the greatest impact on designing our collective legacy and future. Everyday people possess the brilliance to make unique connections and expose formal and informal meanings to concepts that remain elusive to academics and practitioners alike. Key to meaningful community connection is the ability to remember the past and present as well as acknowledge and affirm each person's sacred personhood. Settler colonialism does not leave space for recognition and self-representation; in fact, it actively works to erase and assimilate. In this context, our starting point is to explore the ways in which people have not been able to name, for themselves, who they are and who they want to be. We will return to resistance and refusal in Part II as we explore how we engage with reclaiming our sacred and complex personhood.

Misrecognition and Misrepresentation

> *A child who is not embraced by the village will burn it down to feel its warmth.*
> —AFRICAN PROVERB

Children are the greatest gifts to the world; if we ignore this fact, we are an endangered species. Preparing for the arrival of a child is a village affair that includes all the living creatures, including the birds, trees, and ants. From birth, children are welcomed to the village or community with rituals, and they transition with rites of passage.

One of the most important rituals in many African traditions is the naming ceremony. This ceremony often begins with prayer and songs of praise to welcome the child's spirit into the world. There is transcendent power in names that influences and shapes material, spiritual, and emotional outcomes because African tradition believes words convey symbolic ideas beyond their literal meaning. Our names are how we recognize ourselves and our individuality and community affiliation.

My name, Aida, has given me great purpose and power. The opera *Aida* tells the story of Aida, an Ethiopian freedom fighter and princess who gave her life to free her people and pursue true love. Though her life ended at the hands of the Egyptian empire, she maintained her dignity until the end. I see many parallels in the life of Nubian princess Aida and my own. I draw inspiration from the meaning and story of my name, which influences my feelings, thoughts, and behaviors, but it wasn't always that way for me.

While I was growing up, many white people, adults and children alike, had difficulty pronouncing my name and demonstrated no interest in learning. I naively believed that if my name were easier to pronounce, my white teachers and coaches would show more interest in my development. Turns out, my name wasn't the only reason I had difficulty finding recognition, but it was one of the first ways I noticed I did not belong.

Misrecognition, nonrecognition, and misrepresentation can leave an indelible mark on our sense of worth and can result in us struggling to be recognized by institutions and individuals that are committed to rendering us invisible or subhuman. Psychiatrist Frantz Fanon rigorously studied the role of colonization on the identity of colonized Black people. As he began his exploration, he wrote in *Black Skin, White Masks*: "Since the [white] other was reluctant to recognize me, there was only one answer: to make myself known."

In doing so, Fanon found himself fervently excavating what he referred to as "black antiquity"; he discovered that not only was the white man wrong, but also Black people were not "primitive or subhuman." Instead, Black people belonged to a civilization in its own right—with its own history, values, traditions, and achievements. This discovery, made possible by the path forged by the Negritude poets, left Fanon feeling empowered, confident, and mobilized: it provided him, if only momentarily, with the sense of self-worth, dignity, and respect that the dominant society had not only failed to recognize and deliver but had undercut every step of the way. Subsequently, Fanon was no longer willing to be recognized on terms imposed by the colonizer.

I, too, refuse to be recognized on terms imposed by dominant settler colonial ways. Like many Black people in the US, I believe that long-term misrecognition and misrepresentation of our sacred personhood is a constant and suffocating reality. It wasn't until I became an undergraduate student at University of California, Berkeley, that I learned language to name this experience.

I chose UC Berkeley because of its history of activism with the Free Speech Movement, Vietnam War resistance, and the related activism of the Black Panther Party. I studied political science and was often the only Black person in many of my classes, even in classes with upward of five hundred students. This was not surprising since the overall Black/African student population at the time was only 2 percent and the Native American population was .01 percent. Angry but not deterred, I joined several student groups that protested, lobbied, and fought to repeal California Proposition 209, the colorblind admissions policy, to remedy the remarkably low admission and attraction rate of Black and Indigenous students.

Instead of working to repeal Proposition 209, the University responded by unveiling a recruitment campaign showcasing exemplary Black and other "underrepresented" students. Their campaign included photos and quotes from students who were featured in banners across campus, pamphlets and flyers shared on campus tours and as recruitment collateral, and on the University's website. Students who participated in this campaign, myself included, were misled to believe this publicity would translate to changes in policy and power to admit more Black and Native students. But this lazy, deceptive, and thinly veiled attempt at "representation" and "visibility" was performative at best and exploitative at worst. Not only was this an inauthentic effort, but the administration also completely neglected our student organizing demands.

This kind of transactional "recognition" and "representation" only advanced UC Berkeley's reputation and image and left me feeling exploited and invisible. My college experience was marked by loneliness, confusion, and frustration. Later, I discovered the scholarship of Gerald Taiaiake Alfred, an Indigenous philosopher and writer, who asserted that the very notion of the kind of recognition and representation employed by institutions is and has always been a colonial tactic to serve the settler project by distracting and coopting Indigenous people so they become instruments of their own oppression and exploitation. I learned a valuable lesson; representation without power is not only meaningless, it's harmful.

Thankfully, I had other experiences that saw my humanity. In addition to maintaining a full course load, I also worked two jobs. During the day I took two AC Transit buses from UC Berkeley's campus to my first job, waitressing at a restaurant in Oakland's Jack London Square, then late at night, I would walk to my other job at a jazz club nearby. My coworkers at both jobs were so precious to me. I often felt seen, recognized, and cared for by them, especially the line cooks who made sure I was fed. They recognized my loneliness and invited me into their homes for meals and to celebrate their children's birthdays; a few even insisted on learning how to make Ethiopian injera and wot.

Service work allowed me to connect deeply with others that society misrecognized as invisible or unimportant. I observed and experienced restaurant management's and patrons' disrespect and disregard for those, like me, who labored to serve food and joy to customers. In that work, dignity violations, the subtle but corrosive assaults to one's sense of self, were a daily experience, which primarily manifested in our unseen and unspoken emotional labor of keeping a smile on our faces despite dehumanizing encounters. In the face of these difficulties, I fondly remember our pre-shift and after-hour gatherings as being times of communion when I did not need to wear a figurative mask.

So many of us had hopes and visions beyond our daily work. We all wanted to contribute to Oakland and to the world—some were aspiring rappers who wanted to perform for their turf, others were undocumented parents fighting for a better life for their children, and some were career waiters and cooks who loved meeting new people and bringing joy through food. All of us deserved dignity; we deserved to be affirmed for our sacred personhood and afforded the ability to participate in the workplace and society knowing our identities would be seen, respected, protected, and cherished.

Without a way to name our experiences and ourselves, we can't name our desires. Our fundamental task as people committed to self-determination is to, as bell hooks shared in *Black Looks*, "break with the hegemonic modes of seeing, thinking, and being that block our capacity to see ourselves oppositionally, to imagine, describe, and invent ourselves in ways that are liberatory. Without this, how can we challenge and invite non-black allies and friends to dare to look at us differently, to dare to break their colonizing gaze?" We must acknowledge the ways our spiritual, mental, emotional, and physical well-being have been compromised. We must confront and contest structures and vestiges of domination that involve both the colonized and colonizer.

Echolocation: Using Sounds to See

We have so much to learn from our nonhuman relatives: they are endowed with innovative and visionary ways of being, communicating, navigating, and understanding our world. *Echolocation* is a technique used by some animals to determine the position of objects using sound. Importantly, echolocation involves creatures singing and calling to communicate information about their environments and each other as a way to survive and thrive. When I think about echolocation in this way, I am reminded of the singing and calling in the Black spiritual tradition and how enslaved Africans employed singing and musical expressions in spite of brutal enslavement. Spirituals, jubilees, and sorrow songs were marked by complex rhythms and call and response, a singing technique rooted in West Africa, to create a public conversation. This form of communication was a unique way in which enslaved Africans survived barbaric bondage, maintained oral histories and traditions of their ancestors, and planned rebellion.

Another critical element of sound, particularly the sounds of Blackness, is the feeling the melody or words give you. Whether you stretch out the timing of a song or emphasize a beat, there is a truth and a feeling that the notes can't tell you. The African way is interested in truth, not accuracy. To tell the truth of a song or experience means you might highlight portions or include context to help the listener feel the complexity. It is through this complexity that we can learn the world around us.

Undrowned: Black Feminist Lessons from Marine Animals by poet, activist, and feminist Alexis Pauline Gumbs shares how echolocation can help creatures navigate, identify friend and foe, and learn about the environment around them—all in the darkness. Gumbs describes how some creatures travel, navigate, and communicate:

> Each migration season, humpback whales travel more than ten thousand miles far from land to return to the precise place where they were born.

> African ball-rolling dung beetles, Namibian desert spiders, and southern cricket frogs use the stars of the Milky Way as their compass, just like some of the most courageous members of our own species once used

the constellations to find their way to freedom from the moral cowardice of tyranny: To ensure they were moving northward, migrants on
the Underground Railroad were instructed to keep the river on one
side and "follow The Drinking Gourd"—an African name for Ursa
Major, or The Big Dipper.

Creating a transspecies connection allows us to learn important lessons
such as how bouncing sounds off objects can change our understanding of
where we can go and how we might get there. Recollection, communication, and navigation all contribute to our ability to understand our position
and plan the journey ahead. These practices are important in our quest to
create kinship and should be the foundation of all that we create.

DESIGN: DEFINITIONAL DILEMMA

My first introduction to design was through fashion. As a young Black child,
I used my hairstyle and how I dressed as important ways to see and express
myself. This love of fashion continued into my young adulthood when I
designed my prom dress from the traditional Ethiopian tilet fabric. To me,
design is a way to be intentional about how I curate my appearance; it is a
way to communicate what I value, and clothes are a wearable artifact to
remember who I am.

Style and fashion are a kind of language that can help us unite a social
movement or express our individuality. In a *Women's Wear Daily* article enti-
tled "Dress and Protest," penned by Tara Donaldson, writer Michaela
Angela Davis reminds us that "Black folks like to look good in general.
There's an inherent sense of style because your body was probably the one
small piece of real estate you had some faculty over and some agency."
Let's consider, for example, the fashion of the Black Panther Party or the
Fruit of Islam; these groups dressed to express their mission. The Black
Panthers mostly wore black clothing (specifically Black leather), afros, and
black berets to emphasize their militancy, radicality, and rebelliousness;
such choices also emphasized their mantra "Black Power." The Fruit of

Islam intentionally wore suits and bow ties to demonstrate their dignity and their religious piety in the face of dehumanization.

These styles are not to be confused with uniforms or costumes; rather, they are intentional ways of expressing the self. Telfar Clemens, founder of the Telfar fashion label, built his brand on that premise. He created a vision of fashion that pioneered the deconstruction of gender norms in fashion. With the motto "Not for you—for everyone," each of his designs champions all genders, shades, and backgrounds, anyone who subscribes to the post-identity world he is creating. Although Clemens is a powerful example of a fashion designer changing the game, his is just one of many interpretations of what design is.

So, What Is Design?

Is design a concept, a paradigm, a heuristic device, a methodology, a discipline, a process, a pedagogy, or a theory? Is it an action or an outcome? Is it a tool of settler colonization? Or is design about "improving" colonial products, policies, and programs? Is it weaponized to create harm? Is everything designed?

These are just a few questions I grappled with in my search for clarity and understanding on the definition of design. Faced with an absence of credible sources for the definition, I returned to Black feminist sociologist and writer Patricia Hill Collins's seminal work. She illuminates the critical importance of shared understanding and definitional alignment to terms, like design, that have multiple meanings. In her *Annual Reviews* article "Intersectionality's Definitional Dilemmas," Collins grapples with the definitional dilemma of intersectionality, a concept that has many interpretations, methodologies, political orientations, and practices. She warns that to assume the concept is a fixed body of knowledge creates "[the] definitional dilemma of defining the field neither so narrowly that it reflects the interests of any one segment nor so broadly that its very popularity causes it to lose meaning." Collins goes on to suggest that definitions and shared meaning offer us a starting place from which to begin our exploration rather than the end of an analysis.

The Western way of making meaning commonly results in consulting a dictionary. If we explore the Merriam-Webster definition, we find the following definitions of the words *design* and *designing*:

DESIGN

1: to create, fashion, execute, or construct according to plan: devise, contrive, design a system for tracking inventory

2a: to conceive and plan out in his mind

   He designed the perfect crime.

2b: to have as a purpose: intend

   She designed to excel in her studies.

DESIGNING

1: acting in a calculating, deceitful way

   She was a designing little minx.

Similar: scheming, calculating, conniving, plotting, intriguing, conspiring

What do these definitions suggest about the meaning of design in its current form? Do these definitions represent designs' complete meaning? Who likely created these definitions? What are these definitions missing?

To begin, we will explore how design and the business of design has its roots in colonization and slavery, how it has weaponized the sacred activity of creation, how it has reinforced dominant settler values and lifestyles, and how design limits the power and potential of us all. Together we will grapple with the difficult realities of design in its current form as well as alternative ways of meaning making to generate insight on the past practices of design.

Here are some of the questions we should ask ourselves:

- Who decides if someone is a designer?

- Is Blackness designed?

- Are we Black or African or both?

- Does Blackness exist only in relationship to whiteness?

Designed Whiteness: Whiteness as a Weapon and a Way of Worship

> *Slavery is the ghost in the machine of kinship.*
> —SAIDIYA HARTMAN, academic and writer

The wounded kinship of Black and African people can never forget the atrocities of chattel slavery and its role in creating kin for some people and property of others.

Dispossessing Black families while conceiving of Black people as property requires the idea of whiteness. For descendants of enslavers, connection and inheritance rest on the foundation of people being property and the consequences of that over time.

For some, the idea that whiteness is a powerful and deadly illusion is hard to grasp. When exploring the past and the ongoing power of white supremacy, we notice that whiteness is the reason so many Africans bleach their skin, why many Black women use harsh chemicals to straighten their hair, and why Black people code-switch.

Code-switching can be particularly pernicious for Black people because it mandates that we negotiate and adjust our mannerisms, our ways of talking and being, for white and dominant cultures. In this context, it can be both dignity stripping and dangerous to just be yourself. This danger is exemplified by Maya Angelou in her poem "The Mask" adapted from the 1896 poem by Paul Laurence Dunbar, "We Wear the Mask." The poem and Angelou's performance of it makes it most clear that the Black life and death depend on the mask. Both by metaphor and literal interpretations the mask holds consequences and paradoxes for Black people.

Whiteness requires all who are outside of it to question and modify themselves for a white status quo so that they may survive. In everyday interactions, Black people are constantly navigating whiteness and the white gaze. To be openly Black in public challenges the whiteness's understood and required submission. For many Black people, being unable to adjust for the white gaze can result in serious injury, including death. Whether explicit or subconscious, whiteness has become the global standard most people use to measure worth and status.

Whiteness is not a person; it is the air we breathe. This metaphor helps us visualize the omnipresence and invisibility of whiteness—that it is in everything and everywhere. For those of us in the global majority, those of us who do not identify as white, whiteness displaces us—literally and figuratively. It makes us strangers in our own home and neighborhoods, always searching for ourselves while living in exclusion. Whiteness is a deadly political project that has been a tool used by the powerful to oppress. Given its pervasiveness, whiteness is largely understood, not explicitly defined.

Yet, despite its impact, the invention of whiteness is relatively new, emerging from the Enlightenment period. Originally, whiteness was created as a racial identity to reinforce land ownership (it still continues to operate in this way today). It was a designed social construct to establish an assumed superiority of one group over others. Initially, whiteness meant pale skin color, protestant, and sober. Interestingly, this definition would exclude many people who identify as white today. Take, for instance, people of Irish descent who are now considered white. Not long ago, Irish people were othered and considered outside whiteness. The illusion of whiteness wants us to believe that it is genetic or a permanent classification, but it's not. Whether it's Italians, Greeks, or, more recently, Cubans, along with other white-passing people, whiteness adjusts and transforms to include new "white" people to maintain its power.

This pattern of people "becoming" white is, too, by design. Whiteness is a slippery, parasitic concept that expands and contracts to maintain its domination. Whether intentional or not, whiteness is a construct that facilitates, sustains, and advances systems of oppression and superiority globally—even in places where there are few "white" people, such as in Nigeria, Ethiopia, and many other African nations. In a literal sense, the design of the white race is minimalist, which is what makes it so dangerous. Whiteness demands a binary. In its definition, you are either white or non-white, in or out. Within that binary it is assumed that those who are classified as white are monolithic. This form of reductionist logic intentionally avoids the complexity and nuance of self-identification and community creation.

Whiteness has been the leading way to organize the world. So many powerful countries claim to be a melting pot or an amalgamation of identities and cultures for the purpose of unity. This is a clandestine way of coercing assimilation. I submit that assimilation is one of the most insidious and enduring forms of violence.

Assimilation, to me, is a grieving process where one loses the very essence of themselves for the comfort of acceptance. Whiteness requires assimilation of non-white people in order to achieve "unity." But in these contexts, *unity* means consolidation and combining for the purpose of hegemony or dominance. These places do not invite their inhabitants to come as they are. No, quite the opposite, to enter the melting pot means abandoning their uniqueness, cultures, customs, languages, spirituality, and other important elements of their sacred personhood. Whiteness asserts supremacy; therefore it demands subordination, even by those who are considered white. For this ideology to prevail, everyone must be conditioned to believe in a standard or default—the pale-skinned, land-owning, protestant man and his values and beliefs. The societal conditioning is reinforced and fortified by another social construct, crime. In the United States and Europe, whiteness, settler logic, and exploitation are evident in all facets of life, particularly in its design and in the application of laws—the rules of what is legal and illegal. Laws, policies, and other informal ways of working and communicating are, at their core, about how systems operate and function. In a settler colonial and capitalist society, those rules are defined, designed, and enforced by this prevailing belief that white is right.

Together with colonial paradigms, whiteness works to define non-white people as barbaric, savage, and uncivilized. To further its superiority, whiteness assumes all others were uncultured, uncouth, uneducated, and without religion until they came in (violent) contact with whiteness. In the European context, the limitations and constraints are well evident. Austrian architect Adolf Loos declared in his essay "Ornament and Crime" that the excessive ornamentation he saw occurring in art and design was "primitive," "criminal," "amoral," and "barbarian" and that decoration was for "degenerates." He continued to insist that ornamentation is analogous to arts and crafts from Indigenous children. Loos was unabashed in his perceived racist cultural superiority and he promoted minimalism and modernity as the civilized alternative to the "old ways." This parallels the history of early architects who prioritized scientific thinking and removed ornamental or flowery writing from official texts. If we revisit the parable of the flowering mimosa tree, we begin to notice a pattern of how settler science rejects knowledge that is non-white, Indigenous, and feminist. Of course, it is not by coincidence, but by ironic design, that science (as defined by Europeans) has decided that those objectified are deemed "not objective."

The limitations of design that are built on the illusion of whiteness and its accepted normality ultimately result in exclusionary and myopic results. Take for example, algorithmic bias that is evident in technology products and services. From internet search results to police facial recognition, these technologies are designed with whiteness as their center in both literal and figurative terms. Despite its goal to make people's lives better, algorithms can, in many cases, deliver technological dignity violations and thinly veiled racist behaviors that perpetuate an already flawed system.

Over and over again, Black people, designers, community organizers, and all others who envision new worlds experience the limits of whiteness in design. In the many attempts to redesign public education, we experience the limits of whiteness and the settler imagination, whether it's redesigning the built environment of the classroom or reforming governance to include charter-operated schools. We don't see improvements in education; instead, we see classrooms with better architecture or décor rather than a shift to learning in nature or in the student's own communities. We see investments move from public schools to charter public schools—the same charter schools that often mimic the regimented conditions of residential schools.

Unsurprisingly, these redesigns that are rooted in the premise of reform turn out to be evolved forms of oppression. These long-held beliefs about the illusion of whiteness and its partnership with colonialism and capitalism clandestinely oppress and subjugate the hearts and minds of all people. Our quest to improve, change, or address injustice and oppression can no longer be incremental. Otherwise, we participate implicitly in affirming the illusion of whiteness. Understanding the omnipresence of this foundational flaw in settler society will allows us to think differently about our role in creating alternatives with new centers.

MY OFFERING: REFUSAL FOR RENEWAL

In Part I, we have explored how settler colonialism has violently destroyed so much of our world. It continues to damage our collective memory by disorienting and removing us from our Indigenous knowledge systems resulting in constraints on our collective imagination. Yet and still, those limitations imposed by generational oppression have not stopped us from surviving and thriving. Through it all, we have resisted subjugation and misrecognition, we have refused to accept things as they are, and we have demanded more for ourselves and those to come.

Our capacity to re-member, think critically, and create our lives is fundamental to the work of freedom. We must be willing to confront and wrestle with the heavy labor of critically examining our past and ourselves, beginning with our people, our names, and our identities. Intentionally, this contradicts the colonial way of designing for us or controlling us. This approach refuses moral cowardice. It refuses lazy attempts to engage with people. Instead, we commit to embracing the responsibility to return to right relationship with the land, each other, ourselves, and the future. In pursuing right relations, we employ the Indigenous philosophy and prayer that "all relations" are connected and honored.

In my experience, definitions emerge from iterative, intentional, deep, grassroots, relational, and cultural processes that facilitate meaning and connection through everyday practices. My work and community taught me that if you are living, you can build kinship. Throughout this book, I intend to explore the questions and challenges that are a part of settler ways of knowing. To that end, rather than offering an empirical definition, I am offering my personal definition for your consideration—that creation and kinship are the activities of realizing power, promise, and possibility.

The concepts of creation and kinship are our innate abilities to birth and cultivate creation with intention. These concepts nurture and nurse a seed. They create a place where, once the seed begins to grow into a tree, we care for its roots and the whole tree, enrich the soil, and amplify the sun; where we protect it all from harsh elements. These concepts create the environment, the resources, the very place where we grow. As we explore our past and look forward to the future, we are called to resist, to demand complete freedom, and to design a world where we can reach our full potential and power.

Join me as we explore deliberate resistance as an entrance to freedom.

KEY READINGS

Bason, Christian, and Robert D. Austin. "The Right Way to Lead Design Thinking." *Harvard Business Review.* February 20, 2019. https://hbr.org/2019/03/the-right-way-to-lead-design-thinking.

Berry, Anne H., Kareem Collie, Penina Acayo Laker, Lesley-Ann Noel, Jennifer Rittner, and Kelly Walters (eds.). *The Black Experience in Design: Identity, Expression and Reflection.* New York: Skyhorse Publishing Company, Inc., 2022.

Césaire, Aimé. *Discourse on Colonialism.* New Delhi: Aakar Books, 2018.

Clark, VèVè A. "Developing Diaspora Literacy and *Marasa* Consciousness." *Theatre Survey* 50, no. 1 (May 2009): 9–18. https://doi.org/10.1017/s0040557409000039.

Collins, Patricia H. *Black Feminist Thought: Knowledge, Consciousness, and the Politics of Empowerment.* New York: Routledge, 2000.

———. "Intersectionality's Definitional Dilemmas." *Annual Review of Sociology* 41 (August 2015): 1–20, https://doi.org/10.1146/annurev-soc-073014-112142.

Coulthard, Glen S. *Red Skin, White Masks: Rejecting the Colonial Politics of Recognition.* Minneapolis: University of Minnesota Press, 2014.

Davis, Angela. *Freedom Is a Constant Struggle: Ferguson, Palestine, and the Foundations of a Movement.* Chicago: Haymarket Books, 2016.

———. *Women, Culture and Politics.* New York: Vintage, 2011.

Donaldson, Tara. "Dress and Protest: Fashion Hasn't Been a Bystander in the Black Civil Rights Movement." *Women's Wear Daily.* February 1, 2021. https://wwd.com/feature/protest-fashion-black-civil-rights-black-panthers-blm-1234715312/.

Fanon, Frantz. *Black Skin, White Masks.* London: Penguin Books, 1952.

Gordon, Avery F. *Ghostly Matters: Haunting and the Sociological Imagination.* Minneapolis: University of Minnesota Press, 2008.

Gumbs, Alexis Pauline. *Undrowned: Black Feminist Lessons from Marine Mammals.* Chico, CA: AK Press, 2020.

hooks, bell. *Black Looks: Race and Representation.* New York: Routledge, 1992.

Kelley, Robin D. G. "The Rest of Us: Rethinking Settler and Native." *American Quarterly* 69, no. 2 (June 2017): 267–76. https://doi.org/10.1353/aq.2017.0020.

Kimmerer, Robin W. *Braiding Sweetgrass: Indigenous Wisdom, Scientific Knowledge and the Teachings of Plants*. Minneapolis: Milkweed Editions, 2020.

LaDuke, Winona. *Recovering the Sacred: The Power of Naming and Claiming*. Chicago: Haymarket Books, 2016.

Lame Deer, Richard Erdoes, and Ruth Rosenberg. *Lame Deer, Seeker of Visions*. New York: Simon And Schuster, 2009.

Loos, Adolf. *Ornament and Crime* (1913). New York: Penguin, 2019.

McCormick, Erin. "Survivors of California's Forced Sterilizations: 'It's Like My Life Wasn't Worth Anything.'" *The Guardian*. July 19, 2021. https:// www.theguardian.com/us-news/2021/jul/19/california-forced -sterilization-prison-survivors-reparations.

McKnight, John. *The Careless Society: Community and Its Counterfeits*. New York: Basic Books, 1995.

Morrison, Toni. *Beloved*. London: New York: Vintage, 1987.

———. *Mouth Full of Blood: Essays, Speeches, Meditations*. New York: Vintage, 2020.

Nielsen, Kim E. *A Disability History of the United States*. Boston: Beacon Press, 2012.

Parsons, Rachel. "Anthropology Association Apologizes to Native Americans for the Field's Legacy of Harm." *Scientific American*. February 20, 2024. https:// www.scientificamerican.com/article/anthropology-association-apologizes -to-native-americans-for-the-fields-legacy-of-harm/.

Rhee, Jeong-eun. *Decolonial Feminist Research: Haunting, Rememory and Mothers*. London: Routledge, 2021.

Rodney, Walter. *How Europe Underdeveloped Africa*. New York: Verso, 2018.

Rosenthal, Caitlin. *Accounting for Slavery*. Cambridge, MA: Harvard University Press, 2018.

———. "How Slavery Inspired Modern Business Management." *Boston Review*. August 20, 2018. https://www.bostonreview.net/articles/caitlin-c-rosenthal -accounting-slavery-excerpt/.

Said, Edward W. "Representing the Colonized: Anthropology's Interlocutors." *Critical Inquiry* 15, no. 2 (Winter 1989): 205–25. https://www.jstor.org/stable /1343582.

Simpson, Audra. "On Ethnographic Refusal: Indigeneity, 'Voice' and Colonial Citizenship." *Junctures*. December 9, 2007. https://pages.ucsd.edu/~rfrank /class_web/ES-270/SimpsonJunctures9.pdf.

Tate, Greg. *Everything but the Burden: What White People Are Taking from Black Culture*. New York: Harlem Moon, 2003.

Tuck, Eve, and K. Wayne Yang. "R-Words: Refusing Research." In *Humanizing Research: Decolonizing Qualitative Inquiry with Youth and Communities* by Django Paris and Maisha T. Winn. Thousand Oaks, CA: Sage Publications, Inc., 2014. Accessed at https://methods.sagepub.com/book/humanizing-research -decolonizing-qualitative-inquiry-with-youth-communities/i798.xml.

Walker, Alice. *The Temple of My Familiar*. New York: Amistad, an imprint of HarperCollins Publishers, 2023.

Wa Thiong'o, Ngugi. *Decolonising the Mind: The Politics of Language in African Literature*. London: J. Currey, 1986.

I am David, slaying Goliath

The pebbles I used turned into diamonds

Even when I'm cut, I shine more brilliantly.

—AIDA MARIAM DAVIS

The Parable of the Table

At this hour, when the sun is the highest in the sky and the heat is the heaviest, the village community meets to eat and discuss village decisions. Villagers congregate at a long rectangular table named The Great Table, as they have for generations. Today, four of the villagers—Duma, Twiga, Bata, and Nyuki—are demanding a transformation. Duma is the fastest runner and one of the most formidable animals in the village, but she never roars or raises her voice. Twiga, on the other hand, rarely runs, and with her long-spotted neck, she is the tallest of the group, offering a unique perspective on almost all village matters. Bata is known for her grace and consistency, waddling on all terrains, creating connections with animals on air, land, and water. Nyuki is one of the smallest of the village inhabitants and yet one of the most feared for her sting and her cohesive tribe of winged relatives.

The seat placements were decided long ago when the bigger, stronger animals created the table and assigned the seats. Today, not much has changed, except there are a few more seats at the old rickety table and, once in a while, those new seats are temporarily occupied by smaller and different creatures. On a typical day Duma, Twiga, Bata, and Nyuki watch as the animals feast on the meat of other animals, some of whom were once their friends.

For so many creatures in this village, the meeting at The Great Table instilled fear, trepidation, and confusion. Twiga could not understand why a table would be designed so low; it was as if creatures of her kind were not even considered when it was created. Bata was terrified of the table as she knew many others who went to the table and never returned. Nyuki and other small flying creatures make decisions very differently and have no use for a table. For generations Duma's relatives held the head seat at the table, but she was not offered a seat because she didn't possess four legs like many of her ancestors; instead, she was ignored and not considered a member of the community.

For years, independently, these creatures have asked, begged, and demanded to be included at the poorly constructed Great Table, but today is different. Through a strange turn of events, they have come together in friendship and solidarity to make a new demand. They want a place or places that can feed all the creatures in the village and a way to make decisions that every member of the village can participate in, not just the creatures who can sit in a chair. While these four alone don't have the blueprint for this new village space, they are ready to co-create it.

Tired of asking the bigger animals for acknowledgment, repair of harm, and support, they began to build relationships and learn other ways of existing from the many different creatures in the village. With the trust and vision of so many, Duma, Twiga, Bata, and Nyuki began to design. They learned that high up in the trees and low underground were dynamic communities of creatures; even underwater they met creatures who had colorful thriving kingdoms. Some of these meetings occurred at the height of the night since some animals are nocturnal, some occurred at dawn or sunset. No matter when or where, these creatures living on the periphery were asked to participate in the community.

The very acts of refusing and resisting the table as it was offered and wanting something new attracted hundreds of other creatures, some of whom had not been seen in hundreds of years. After meeting all of these new creatures, these four unlikely friends were fundamentally changed.

This was just the beginning of the journey. They realized so much more needed to be changed, and not just the table.

The metaphor of the table represents the many ways humans and nonhumans gather and experience each other. The table is not a benign object in this parable; in fact, far from it. The long rectangular shape, the height of the table, its location, the seat arrangement, and the number of seats—all were designed with only a few powerful creatures in mind. Tacit decisions and understandings of who eats and speaks first, the cultural importance and value of designated seats, and the historical context are all important design considerations and contribute to the condition of The Great Table.

Those creatures who had seats for generations had no reason or incentive to rethink The Great Table since it served their needs and interests. While a table can be myopically or meticulously designed only for the powerful, that is not it's only purpose. For many African and Indigenous peoples, a table represents a place to gather to offer kinship, friendship, rituals, and nourishment. It is a place used to facilitate celebrations like Kwanzaa and routines like weekly Sunday dinners. Matters of intergenerational importance and everyday joy occur tableside.

For Duma, Twiga, Bata, and Nyuki, the table represents violence, brutality, and exclusion. Merely including them at a table designed for their consumption and invisibility does not structurally make that table *better* or desirable for them. The four creatures realize that a table that is poorly designed is a table that they do not want to join or be seated at. In an act of defiance to the status quo and to gain dignity for themselves and others, they set out to create something new with other village creatures.

The Great Table, a table that governs and feeds so many, ignored and erased the sacred dignity and the being of many seen and unseen creatures. We must ask ourselves, was this the only or best way to build a community?

PART II

REFUSE

UNSETTLE
THE SETTLER

Sawubona.
Yebo Sawubona!

Translation: We see you.
I see you seeing me!

Resistance is a refusal to take on outsider interpretations of our lives. Resistance and refusal often require us to first see ourselves and then act in accordance with our natural selves so that we do not succumb to suffering. It is the mimosa tree that is scarred from its experiences but not broken, the tree that sustains the possibility of creation by just existing.

For as long as I can remember, I have considered myself a radical. Someone who grasps challenges by the root and accepts the societal stigma of not conforming.

When I became a labor and community organizer, I developed and transformed my radical theory and praxis to build relationships across differences with the shared values of dignity, care, and community. Similarly, the Zulu greeting and concept of *Sawubona* speaks to this shared humanity—our inherent desire to want to be understood and valued for who we are. The beauty of this greeting is experienced by the communal and figurative nature of sight. The greeting, "we see you," demonstrates a warmth, comfort, and safety in being seen in the everyday activities of our life. To be acknowledged for who we are, and not what society identifies us as, is a powerful way to externally orient ourselves.

In her poem "Revolutionary Dreams," poet Nikki Giovanni offers us a prophetic vision of resistance that ventures beyond protest and "perceptive powers"; she invites us to reflect deeply on our true essence and then be that person. It is only then, she claims, that we will have the revolution we desperately need and want. This poem has been, and continues to be, paradigm shifting for me. Imagine resistance not as a violent or coercive experience, but rather as a return to who we are in our natural state without seeking anyone's permission. In remembering this wisdom, I am called to explore my inner world and reflect on who I am, what my values are, and who my people are. I am reminded that our true essence and being, both colonized and settler, are not defined by settler colonialism or capitalism but rather impacted and influenced by it. This understanding of resistance and revolution as a return to our sacred selves is intentional work that often manifests as struggle.

This struggle is the daily labor of community organizers and activists— to facilitate conversations and guide the exploited and oppressed to find themselves and each other in order to build power to resist oppressive social and political structures, vestiges and institutions of colonialism. Whether in the workplace or on your block, organizers resist oppression by building deep intentional relationships of trust and accountability through time, proximity, and care. The disciplined labor and love of organizers inspire us and remind us that it is not enough to change systems and institutions; the real work of transformation is knowing ourselves and each other—the internal revolution. As organizers, we know that if you can transform yourself, you can transform the world. If you make choices that align with your values, then people and the planet will transform.

One of the most transformational labor union campaigns I've worked on was in the small community of SeaTac, Washington, home to many immigrant, working-class people. In 2013, the city of SeaTac proposed a campaign for an ordinance that would establish the first living wage of $15 an hour and paid sick leave campaign in the United States. This proposition was put on the ballot through the efforts of airport workers who were mostly recent immigrants from Ethiopia, Eritrea, and Somalia. As we began our Get Out the Vote (GOTV) efforts, many of the workers resisted door-to-door agitation and fact sharing of the proposition. These traditional union campaign tactics were textbook labor-organizing tactics, ones that focused on discovering people's individual self-interest and taking direct action on that self-interest. While effective in some settings, these tactics were not compatible with the kinship culture and traditions of East Africans.

This campaign was the first where I spoke Amharic to organize workers who, much like my parents and relatives had been, were new immigrants to the US. One of the first doors I knocked on was that of an elderly, single Ethiopian woman who I affectionately called *Eteye* (which is a respectful and endearing way to address elders in Amharic). She insisted I come in and join her for a coffee ceremony so that we could talk *sineserat* (translation: in a dignified fashion) about winning the campaign. She lit frankincense, roasted raw coffee beans, and then sat on the ground to pop popcorn in a pan and brew the coffee on a portable camp-style burner. She refused all my campaign-related questions and redirected to inquire about me and my family. It was clear she was the real organizer, not me. I stopped trying to mobilize her and instead spent two hours talking with her about her life growing up in Gondar, Ethiopia, her difficult immigration to the US, and her very active church life. Though elderly herself, she worked as an airport wheelchair service agent for disabled and elderly passengers. She loved her job and coworkers, and like most people, needed the income to survive. Yet and still, her job did not define her or her potential, or give her communal connection or personal meaning.

She joked about how Ethiopians born here, like me, lived to work, and how we were so book smart and game goofy. In other words, we understood the American ways of the world but didn't understand life. After spending the afternoon with her, during which time we spoke very little about the campaign itself, she offered to take me to her church to introduce me to other workers and she offered to make an announcement to the congregation about the campaign.

With so much to lose—from being fired, to being deported, or worse—these workers understood the gravity of their campaign and remained steadfast to our grassroots efforts. I was in awe of their fearlessness, their defiance, and the urgency with which they demanded better from their employer. In the face of pervasive employer intimidation, the wallpaper of propaganda in break rooms, and the constant loop of anti–living wage commercials that played on their radios and televisions in their homes, they resisted. This continued for a few months, but still, despite our round-the-clock organizing efforts, we were not sure if this ordinance would pass.

As the votes were tallied, and I paced anxiously, Eteye reminded me of the Ethiopian proverb: "If there is no enemy within, the enemy outside can do no harm." She was suggesting that no matter the outcome, as long as we were sineserat, we would not be harmed. Western cultures believe people live for a purpose and profit; this contradicts Ethiopian culture, which suggest people are like nature—alive and aware—we don't need anything to achieve our worth and humanness. I doubt Eteye ever read Nikki Giovanni's poem, but she embodied the message effortlessly, that being natural herself could bring revolutionary change. The serendipitous encounter in which she brought me into her world, and in many ways organized me, revolutionized how I understood my role as organizer. The historic passage of Proposition 1 raised not only the wages of these immigrant workers, but also their hopes, self-confidence, spirit, and consciousness—and it raised mine as well.

COMMUNITY DESIGN: PARENT INNOVATION INSTITUTE

It is important to first acknowledge the Ohlone land, known by many as Oakland, and the people who inhabit it as I tell you about the creation of the Parent Innovation Institution. Oakland, California, raised me. Though I was not born there, many of my most formative experiences occurred during my fifteen years living in Oakland. The birthplace of the Black Panther Party for Self-Defense and countless other movements for freedom and justice, Oakland taught me how to organize and exercise my power, how to struggle and resist the status quo, and how to cultivate deep relationships to move mountains. I attended the School of Unity and Liberation (SOUL) in addition to my college education, and during my time in Oakland, I met and learned from elders and movement leaders like Chairperson Elaine Brown, Congressperson Barbara Lee, and Harry Belafonte, to name a few. I am forever indebted to the people, hoods, and campaigns that poured into me and held me accountable. But my time there was not without adversity.

I was twenty years old, living and working in West Oakland, when I first saw someone get shot in broad daylight in an elementary school garden. I was twenty-four, working deep in East Oakland when I saw a police officer shoot an unarmed Black high school student in an attempt to break up a fight. I was twenty-nine when I lived and lounged on Lake Merritt, where one day BBQ Becky harassed and then called the police on a group of Black people cooking and relaxing in a public place. This instance very likely could've been a deadly encounter for those Black people.

The culture, context, and characteristics of the Oakland community are critical details in understanding the intention and impact of the Parent Innovation Institute. The institute was a co-owned and codesigned experience that I had the honor of facilitating in 2017. In late 2015, I was recruited to re-create and direct a design thinking initiative in East Oakland to very generally "create better early learning services" for low-income families. Originally named the Parent Success Collaborative, the initiative's theory of change was that parents should be asked their thoughts on current government services and outside consultants and staff should create prototypes on the parents' behalf. I was repulsed by the paternalistic notion that outside consultants would create for, not with, communities. More than that, I was skeptical that creating program improvements to bureaucratic programs and services would produce results for families in real time. Working in and around bureaucracies, I've seen how competent communities have been occupied and colonized by professionalized services—often with violent results. In a context like the United States, this looks like prejudiced bureaucrats and administrators leading communities without responsibility or limit. This in turn results in arrests, deportations—family separation for Black and Indigenous peoples.

When I joined, the initiative was already staffed with a design thinking consultant. She was a white woman from Boston who openly disregarded my lived experience and background as a community organizer and, more importantly, the lived experience of parents and families in East Oakland. During her first and only visit to Oakland, to meet me and the community members interested in the initiative, she insisted on the experience being facilitated exclusively by an expert, namely herself, and that the approach maintain design purity. Confused by the concept of design purity, I asked her for an explanation, for myself and the group, and in response, I received an exasperated and dismissive reply that I interpreted as further reinforcing the notion that design is inaccessible and unavailable to people like us. She hinted at the idea that only a select few understand the design process and only they should be trusted to create prototypes. She wanted us to understand how prestigious and elite her process was. She went on to highlight her plan to do ethnographic research on the families and the larger East Oakland community. One mother, unfamiliar with the concept of ethnographic research, asked what that meant, and the consultant's response was "I will study what you do and how you do it so that I can help you be a better parent."

I was shocked. How dare she assume these families needed help becoming "better parents"? She had just met them. Who should become better parents? Why did she assume these families needed help with parenting? What parenting standards was she referencing? Did she know that many of these parents worked three jobs to provide for their families? Did she know about Oakland's rapid gentrification that was deliberately displacing friends, neighbors, and relatives because they couldn't afford the rent? Did she know the ways these families parent and raise children together? Did she know about the raids by US immigration officers at peoples' workplaces and homes that caused many undocumented people to live in the shadows? How did she not know that kinship and family are the center of African, Black, and Indigenous life? She'd never lived in California, let alone Oakland, and she certainly did not know the lived experience of being Black, Mexican, undocumented, a monolingual Spanish speaker, or illiterate. Most importantly, she was unable to recognize her settler ideology, that she viewed those who did not share her identity and point of view as deficient or inferior.

Many of the parents in the Parent Innovation Institute struggled economically because their neighborhoods were designed to maintain poverty, not because they did not care about their children. I knew this because I had spent months doing relational meetings with families and community members to learn about their experiences, hopes, dreams, and visions for themselves and their families. I had earned trust and learned the incredible personal stories of many of the parents in the room that day.

The consultant's world view and approach to partnering with the community was not compatible with the kind of experience or the community we envisioned. I explained to her that the implicit and inherent deficit framing of the experiences of families would not work for this initiative. While she enthusiastically disagreed with my decision, I began to consider what this experience would feel like if we didn't have a "design thinking expert."

Before I could indulge in a truly community-centered design alternative, another consultant was hired, this time a white woman who was a lecturer at the Stanford d.school. This woman spent even less time meeting with the families in the neighborhood and focused primarily on creating a curriculum that would introduce community members to design. We held our first workshop at the Eastside Arts Alliance, a community art space in the Fruitvale neighborhood of Oakland.

Fruitvale is a primarily Spanish-speaking community that borders several Black neighborhoods. The morning of the workshop, I met the consultant at 7 a.m. to prepare the space. At around 7:15 a.m., an elderly Black man walked in to check out the Black Panther exhibit in the space of our workshop. I welcomed him to the space and explained that at around 9 a.m. we would be using the space to run a workshop. I stepped away for about ten minutes to use the bathroom, and when I returned, the consultant let me know she asked him to leave because he looked, as she described, "sketchy." Although I was offended by her characterization of his appearance, I decided this was not worth my energy this early in the morning, and I proceeded to arrange donuts.

In the time it took to turn my back and pick up the first donut, I heard the consultant yell, "He stole my wallet!" She was referring to the elderly Black man who had come to tour the art. I was shocked by the accusation and confused as to how she knew that man had stolen it. I asked her to retrace her steps, but she refused. She insisted that she was certain the man had stolen it and that she had to call the police to retrieve it. I begged her not to call and walked with her to her car to check to see if it was there. As soon as we could see inside the car, we saw the wallet. She had forgotten that she had taken out the wallet to pay the meter on the street. She was visibly relieved but said nothing about her accusation or impulse to call the police on that elderly Black man. Her panic, fear, and lack of care for the Black man could have resulted in him being handcuffed or worse. Rather than taking responsibility for her mistake, she continued the day as if nothing had happened.

Although this incident on its own was distressing, it was just a precursor to what would be her last day working for the Parent Innovation Institute. On that day, during our first breakout session, the consultant joined a group of mothers who were coming up with ideas on how to make reading more accessible for monolingual or illiterate parents. The consultant was visibly disturbed by the fact that some parents did not speak English.

I enthusiastically encouraged the parents to speak in their mother tongue, and I embraced the many different ways they offered to engage with their children, in spite of designed institutional barriers. Interestingly, at no point did the mothers offer the idea that those who didn't speak English should learn so they could read to their children in English. Instead, they explored writing their own children's books in Spanish or Mam, an Indigenous language of Central Americans.

Frustrated with the direction of the conversation, the consultant demanded that all the breakout groups stop and take her direction, which was to come up with ideas on how they could be better parents and improve themselves. It was clear to me that she did not believe that these parents could be self-determined and that they could define themselves for themselves. It was also clear she was a violent person who did not have any regard for the psychological and physical safety of others, particularly those most vulnerable. Her behavior and beliefs were consistent with those "design experts" who continue the pattern of harm the settler colonizers before them imposed. As a result of this experience, and many other experiences working alongside communities, I began to be outspoken in my critiques of design thinking and continue to co-create alternatives; our communities' safety depends on it.

DESIGN THINKING OR TAKING?

You must understand that for people like us, there are no such things as models. We are called upon to constantly create our models. For African people, Africans in the diaspora, it's pretty much the same. Colonialism means that we must always rethink everything.
—OUSMANE SEMBÈNE, Senegalese filmmaker

I giggled the first time I heard the words *human-centered design*. Why did practitioners of design thinking need to remind themselves of the humanity of those they were designing for? Does putting *human* in the name of the process remind them to see the humanity of others?

I was first exposed to design thinking in graduate school. It was evangelized as the most innovative way to solve complex problems. Not long after
I learned about design thinking, I learned that the people who experienced
its products and services were called *users*. Before being introduced to design,
I had only heard the term *user* in reference to people addicted to substances
or otherwise controlled by outside entities, like in video games. The more
I explored the concepts of design thinking, the more questions I had. By
using specific methods with prescribed mindsets, design thinking intends to
improve products, programs, and policies. Many corporations, universities,
and other institutions employ this problem-solving approach to find new
ways to maximize profits while exploring solutions for unknown problems.

We are led to believe the methodology of design thinking was founded
by white men. Some people place the founding of design thinking in the
early 1900s and others mark its inception to coincide with the proliferation of the practice in the mid-1980s. No matter when you mark the start,
today the methodology has been used by countless companies, organizations, and institutions as a primary way to innovate. Unsurprisingly, design
thinking continues the settler colonial pattern of defaulting to white Eurocentric norms and values that are predicated on superiority, theft, denial,
and harm. Design thinking, much like other processes created by settlers for
settlers, has been elitist, exploitative, exclusionary, and extractive. Explicitly, design thinking aims to improve peoples' quality of life. Implicitly, it is
paternalistic in that it assumes a default standard for ones' quality of life,
that the designer knows the best lifestyle, and that the designer can discover
the intimate and unspoken desires of the user. Moreover, design thinking
assumes that there is a deficit and improvement is not a self-determined
experience, instead it is one that is universal and objective. As we've seen
in our exploration of settler colonialism, it is clear that this point of view
has become a vehicle for coercing assimilation and that it has created the
conditions for abuse.

Allegedly design thinking is rooted in the mindsets of curiosity and
thinking big, and yet, inquiry and ideation, key steps in the design thinking
process, seem to be constrained by significant limitations. For instance, I
once participated in a panel with leading designers and we were asked how

we might redesign cities to better accommodate the diversity of the people in our communities. All of the panelists responded with either a process or way of thinking about varied ways cities can operate to accommodate differences. Though realistic, the responses maintained the status quo and did not question the very structure and system that cities are built on.

The most glaring question to me is not whether cities need improvement, it is whether cities in their current form are serving the different people who inhabit them. In other words, the question becomes this: Do we even need to organize ourselves in cities? Further, when we talk about improvement or making things "better," who decides what those words mean and how those words are implemented? Does *better* mean more efficient? As we've seen in the examples I gave about working with consultants, that usually comes at an exploitative cost. On the other hand, having the luxury to indulge the radical imagination, particularly of the oppressed, requires a kind of time and lifestyle free from violence and distraction that is unavailable to many Black and Indigenous peoples. To me, this is one of the greatest offenses of settler colonialism: the subjugation of the colonized imagination and free time.

In the same 2019 *Harvard Business Review* design thinking article I mentioned in "The Fourth L: Labor" in Part I, the authors emphasize the mandate of participants of design thinking to "repeatedly experience" failure. Although it is true that settler Eurocentric norms value perfectionism and discourage mistakes and failure, it is also true that failure does not have the same costs for everyone. For Black and similarly oppressed peoples, there is a short runway for error and the results cost a lot more than for other groups, sometimes with deadly consequences. In one Parent Innovation Institute workshop, a single mother gave voice to this point poignantly. She said in Spanish, "I reject this idea of failing often. If I create something here that gets too much attention, I can be deported. My small children need me and I won't gamble my current situation for this experiment." We cannot assume universal mindsets or ways of thinking, and it's irresponsible to evangelize them to others with more to lose. More importantly, failure has to be put in context. We can't forget that we are living in a world and context where some people are oppressed, neglected, and dehumanized.

The settler dominant norms and default Eurocentric worldview create the conditions for false assumptions, misappropriation, and misinterpretation. This is especially obvious in the design thinking community where unintended consequences are dismissed or denied. For instance, think about technology and products that use facial recognition, like those popular on many phones; at first, these technologies were unable to recognize darker-skinned faces since they were designed and developed by white technologists. Alternatively, facial recognition has been weaponized against dark-skinned people as it has become a tool for mass surveillance and racial profiling by police and law enforcement. The dismissal and trivializing of these consequences often amount to loss of life and liberty for Black people.

Much has been written by designers about the harms and shortcomings of design, and many world-renown designers have been outspoken about the racist, misogynistic, and ableist gatekeeping within the practice; they also relate how white settler supremacist norms and values are reinforced by the harmful and irreversible damage of "unintended" consequences. This harm extends beyond the design community to everyday people who want to create a world where we all thrive.

My personal experience in design has been reinforced by the ongoing shortcomings of and harmful interactions with designers. In a conversation with an executive from the large design firm IDEO, I felt accosted by leading questions that left me with little time or space to develop a relationship with him. The interaction began with my counterpart firing off questions like this:

"You can't be serious that you really want to 'decolonize' design?"

"What are your design credentials, and where did you go to school?"

"I don't think you understand the nuance of this work. Do you really think this is the work your organization should focus on?

"I read your background is in community organizing. I am very interested in incorporating that into design; can I pick your brain about that?"

I felt like I was in an interrogation. I was being mined for information and was receiving passive-aggressive jabs all while my expertise was being undermined. In the moments following the exhausting conversation, I received an email from the IDEO executive requesting even more information similar to the questions he had asked, without acknowledging or compensating me for what I had already shared—an expectation I am sure he would enforce as an executive of a large company himself.

I can only guess that this IDEO executive believed he was being curious and employing a tried-and-true design research method in our conversation, commonly referred to as *inquiry*. But his approach showed no interest or attempt to acknowledge or explore other ways of knowing or cultural orientations. Because he neglected me, the subject of the inquiry, I never gave him any answers; instead, I met his approach with refusal and subversion.

A NOTE ON REFUSAL AND RESISTANCE

The only place where Black people did not revolt is in the pages of capitalist historians.

—C. L. R. JAMES, historian; from the essay "Revolution and the Negro"

To refuse is a form of love. Love for yourself, love for others, love for a world that doesn't love you back. Black people in the diaspora have never accepted subjugation and domination. We, Black and African people, have refused, rebelled, resisted, and revolted at every opportunity, and we've survived the unthinkable. We know this to be true because of artifacts and the intergenerational oral tradition of our elders. This is the primary role of a *griot*. Griots are sacred keepers of past stories, songs, poems, genealogies, wisdom, and traditions. Typically, griots are village or community elders who train and spend their lives listening to stories and songs from generations before. Though most commonly associated with West African men, this sacred role has many names across the African diaspora and is occupied by all genders. Today, these historians/storytellers take many forms such as rappers, poets, activists, scholars, or your neighborhood barber. These griots archive accounts and interpretations of past and present resistance that are the lifeline and inspiration we need to continue to realize deep kinship and connection.

Here, in this text, I am continuing the tradition of preserving and sharing the erased, denied, and ignored histories, stories, songs, and analyses of everyday and grand-scale resistance. Much like design, resistance faces a definitional dilemma. I've learned that resistance tends to be contextual and personally defined. I submit to you, the reader, that *resistance* is a deep understanding and connection to yourself that in turn produces intentional action or inaction. In this section, we explore some of the ways to employ resistance for individual and collective freedom.

It is important for me to mention that refusal and resistance frequently manifest in moments of violence, terror, and trauma. Choosing to resist can be the difference between physical, psychological, and spiritual life or death. During the trial of a white former police officer who was convicted of the murder of George Floyd, Donald Williams, a witness to Floyd's murder, described the terror and violence he saw as Floyd's last breaths slowly escaped his body. Williams testified and said, "I stayed in my body," repeatedly. Despite the prosecution's best efforts to paint Williams, a Black man, as angry and recalcitrant, he resisted those characterizations. And when the prosecution went so far as to suggest he should have neglected his own body to stop the terror inflicted by the police officer, Williams resisted. He refused to participate or respond to the prosecution's offensive line of questioning, and most importantly, he refused to abandon himself in his own suffering and pain.

Violence and violation are key characteristics of settler colonialism's abusive design and nature. To return to right relationship with land, language, lifestyle, and labor, we must prioritize the survival and persistence of Black and African people, at all costs. That pursuit has historically produced violence, whether out of self-defense, self-preservation, or protection. We will not explore in great detail violent resistance, though I acknowledge its role as a response to exploitation, subjugation, and other forms of violence.

Refusal and resistance can be tools for temporary change. In a capitalist and colonial system that is designed and rigged to benefit elite groups, superficial resistance can provide short-term relief, at best, and more long-term destruction at worst. For instance, the mass resistance to state-sanctioned violence after the highly publicized murders of Breonna Taylor and George Floyd has been followed by another thousand (and counting) state-sanctioned murders with no mass resistance or response.

Without a deep understanding and analysis of our systems, resistance turns into a performance. So, the difference between resisting for dignity and resisting for reformist efforts is learning how to think critically, act with intention, and connect to a vision of freedom.

Here we will explore refusal and resistance in their many forms including, but not limited to, silence, rest, refusal, and rage. These concepts trigger a variety of responses in people. For some, resistance is a tool for liberation and for others resistance can create the conditions for domination. We will explore what these concepts mean in different settings to Black and oppressed people in a settler context. In this context, resistance is stigmatized and criminalized; for the oppressed, however, resistance presents opportunities for self-generated insight and power to design and decolonize. I am asking that we, you and I, widen our aperture and grapple with these concepts in a new way. In other words, consider the following narratives and perspectives not to be directives but to be inspiration for everyday ways we can choose to refuse and resist—how we can choose sovereignty of our minds, bodies, and spirits in the face of settler colonialism.

In the following pages, we will explore the many ways we can, and do, resist colonization and capitalist designs.

Let us consider and embrace resistance in its complexity.

ROOTS OF RESISTANCE: DEFINING YOURSELF FOR YOURSELF

True resistance begins with people confronting pain and wanting to do something to change it.
—bell hooks, *Yearning: Race, Gender, and Cultural Politics*

Resistance has special value in the journey to reconnect with kin and efforts to create anew because it represents the embodied imagination, the

concerted learning, and the defiant action of the oppressed. More specifically, in the settler socioeconomic-political context, it is our refusal to accept
the material and spiritual conditions as they are.

The unsettling, resisting, and defying of the settler status quo is not just
an external fight, it is the internal struggle to define yourself in an evolving
context. No one has more proximity to your lived experience than you. No
one understands the defining experiences, memories, trauma, joy, and circumstances that led you to where you are today—no one but you.

Many of us have been assigned, conditioned, and in some cases forced
to accept identities that don't align with our true selves. Settler colonial
knowledge systems and binaries produce anti-Black, racial, gendered, and
"normal" ways of understanding ourselves and imagining the world. Doing
the labor and taking the time to explore yourself is the foundation of resistance. Plainly put, you must know who you are in order to resist. So, our
work as Black people, designers, leaders, activists, and community members
begins with the labor of undoing the systems through which knowledge is
created and understood.

Oppression has defined the settler colonizer condition. For some people,
their oppression has become a defining part of their identity; for others it
has led to self-deception and disillusionment. In both cases the psychological harm is more damaging than what meets the eye. For instance, let's consider food systems in Black and Indigenous communities in America. These
communities were designed to lack access to healthy and affordable food,
thereby becoming neglected poor communities. This intentional city design
is harmful for many reasons but one is the long-term cognitive damage
that results from malnutrition. *Food apartheid*, designing systems and conditions that restrict food sovereignty and access, coupled with the normalized,
omnipresent, ongoing violence of settler colonialism can impair and dis-
tract our natural and innate capacities to face these harsh circumstances in
order to resist.

Resisting settler colonialism, and other forms of oppression, is the foundation of reclaiming our sacred nature as humans. Refusing to comply or
accept ways of knowing, being, and doing disrupts the normative operation
of settler colonialism. Exploring past and present patterns of settler colonialism offers us clarity on how it appears in our lives. By refusing the notion

that the United States was "discovered" by Christopher Columbus or by refusing to work with a company that has exploitative and discriminatory business practices, we resist—first acknowledging and then refusing to participate in these patterns' proliferation.

Following the vision of Frantz Fanon, Sylvia Wynter, a Jamaican anti-colonial philosopher and novelist, offers us a perspective rooted in settler colonial intellectual disobedience. In almost all of Wynter's writing, she asks us to step outside of a system that fails to notice our stories and humanity. She invites us on a journey to explore evolving ourselves. In an essay he contributed to the book *Sylvia Wynter: On Being Human as Praxis*, professor and semiotician Walter D. Mignolo explores her work's profound impact on how we might consider ourselves and our own humanity:

> Wynter suggests that if we accept that epistemology gives us the princi-ples and rules of knowing through which the Human and Humanity are understood, we are trapped in a knowledge system that fails to notice that the stories of what it means to be Human—specifically origin stories that explain who/what we are—are, in fact, narratively constructed.

Wynter recognizes that we do not exist in isolation; in fact, we exist in a distinct context and community story that helps us understand our human-ity. This decolonial pedagogy calls us to take time to know who we are, free from our assigned and forced identities—and this exploration of who we are in our essence is the foundation of all resistance. The opportunity to turn our attention to an internal exploration allows us to bloom and natu-rally resist the dominant narrative of who we were/who we are.

Some of the first questions we must ask ourselves are these:

- Who am I?

- Who will I be?

- Who was I?

- Who are my people?

- What experiences shape(d) or define(d) me?

- What is important that people see and know about me, literally and figuratively?

CHILD'S PLAY

These questions we ask ourselves are not answered once. In many African traditions, these questions are ceremony. They are routine and ritualized since they amount to the defining questions of our existence as humans. Exploring our many identities and experiences in fullness without constraints or compartmentalization is in itself an act of remembering and resisting. My resistance to colonization has always been motivated by children and the unborn. Becoming a parent has offered me a window into who I am (and who I am not) and who I can be. Through my children's wonder and exploration of the world I witness what it feels and looks like to be human without subjugation, domination, or exploitation by others. I've learned from them the serious and disciplined activities of wonder and play.

That said, the concept of play and learning from children has become a trite and overused idiom that, in practice, turns out to be superficial at best, and paternalistic at worst. The desire to learn from a child, or anyone, should be motivated by respect and a desire to deepen the relationship beyond that moment. In other words, when we learn from others, we must see and assume their brilliance and humanity and reject societal conditioning on worthiness and formal knowledge. How we treat our children, not just the ones related to us, shows us what we believe about our future. When we believe that children should be seen and not heard we are saying that children are fixtures without thoughts or feelings that require attention or care. Alternatively, when we believe children are gifts that are sacred and full of feelings, we are suggesting that we must attend to them and guide them because we are their stewards.

Most children do not comprehend or show any interest in understanding societal confines or binaries; they question the way things are incessantly and see the world around them as having limitless possibilities. Through loving relationships and play children learn, imagine, care, and become very conscious of the world around them.

Even as young as a year old, children have a lot to teach us. While writing this book, I took a break to play with my daughter and her shape-sorting cube, a toy box in the shape of a cube with designed openings for other smaller-shaped objects to fit through. To begin, I showed her a few times how each shape fits neatly in the cube and I put a few in the box with her, then I handed over the rest for her to figure out. She looked at the box, then at the shapes on the ground, then back at the box, then around the room— as if she needed to figure out the use and purpose of the box separate from my demonstration.

After a few minutes of observing and wondering, she began to shake the box. She noticed the sound and movement of the small pieces in the box, but she had a greater vision for the box than sorting. By shaking the box, she released the top slat and pulled it clean off. Once she opened the box completely, she began to put all the smaller pieces in the box. Watching her confidently explore and experiment with the box was a serious lesson I think about regularly. Moving beyond the cliche, "putting a square peg in a round hole," my child refused the premise of a "round hole" or that pegs need to enter the box sequentially. She embodied out-of-the-box thinking (pun intended) by opening the box, exploring the box and its relationships to the smaller objects, and finally putting them together in an arrangement that she defined. This moment taught me to resist my impulse to "train" my child, or assert my authority and direction, and instead embrace her resistance to doing as I instructed. She effortlessly showed me creative thinking and refused to compromise.

When children don't comply or they resist direction, we begin to problematize the situation and, over time, that turns into problematizing the child. When children disrupt the ceremonial order of things, or ways of doing, parents become concerned, not just about their child's development, but that their child might be considered or labeled different than other children. My daughter's natural resistance to doing things the way they have always been done is instinctive behavior that should be engaged with, nurtured, and cultivated. If we take the time to observe, listen, and respect them, this is one of the many ways children can teach us and show us alternative ways of being and doing. We can create relationships predicated on *cognitive justice*, a term coined by scholar Shiv Visvanathan, the understanding that there are many ways to express knowledge and that the different forms can all coexist. This paradigm shift allows parents and children to reverse the colonial relationship of domination. Engaging with children in this manner is an everyday way to build new ways of relating.

REST AND RETREAT AS RESISTANCE

To that end, another important, dare I say the most important, way we resist can be learned from the youngest of children—resting.

The Nap Ministry

One thing about capitalism and colonialism that remains persistent over time, place, and space is the subversive theft of rest and leisure time in the name of productivity and profit. Under these two systems, the lifegiving acts of rest, sleep, daydreaming, and unplugging are believed to be wasteful, unnecessary, and potentially costly to our socioeconomic status and advancement—arguably by mechanical design. If we recall the conditions of settler colonialism, specifically enslavement and extermination, we see nonstop work experiences that were the literal manifestations of a no-rest, survival-first environment. Predictably, this pattern continues today with the romanticized hustle-and-grind culture that values nonstop work and productivity. Moreover, we see the impact this kind of environment has on mental, physical, and spiritual health and on increasing levels of the stress hormone cortisol. These systems lead to the individual literally compromising their ability to simply connect with others and dream.

Therefore, silence and stillness are formidable forms of resistance, particularly to the violence of a settler society not designed with Black and Indigenous people in mind, or worse, designed to oppress them. In an evolved settler state, there is an unspoken expectation that we educate or articulate to the powerful our experiences and, more importantly, that we assert our dignity. Resistance as rest is about restorative silence and healing. It is where we can experience the supernatural and understand that the paradox of stillness is a kind of holy movement.

One organization leading the movement on rest and rejuvenation for the liberation and redemption of our spirit is The Nap Ministry, founded by

Tricia Hersey. She has designed a sacred gathering space called Resurrect Rest School dedicated to the deep study, teaching, and practice of The Nap Ministry's rest-as-resistance framework. According to their website,

> The School serves as an intensive intervention and provocative space to understand and embody *The 4 Tenets of The Nap Ministry*, a series of core principles "infused with the principles of Black Liberation Theology, Afrofuturism, Womanism, somatics, and communal care."

This kind of insurgent and sacred space creates the climate and infrastructure for rehabilitating the weary and tired.

Hersey warns us that rest must not be a way to rejuvenate to be more productive for the systems of exploitation. So much of who we are and who we can be is defined by our ability to produce and labor that the obsession with productivity and profit has created a moral, emotional, spiritual, physical, and intellectual deficiency in ourselves and our systems. Resistance, as rest or refusal, asks us to move beyond productivity and profit-driven outcomes and begins to define who we are, who we want to be, and what we want to create, in spite of our circumstances. Embodied resistance as rest can appear in the everyday ways we dress and do our hair (or not!). Black women have long been policed and punished for their natural hair. Hairstyles like the Afro, braids, twists, Bantu knots, or locs are stigmatized and in settler context associated with "rebels." However, in the African or Black tradition, these hairstyles are not only natural, they are beautiful. Resistance as rest calls all of us to opt out of the white ideals, including Eurocentric standards of beauty, and enjoy our natural state, including our hair. The role of hair for Black and Indigenous peoples continues to be intrinsic to self-definition, self-expression, and liberation.

Refuse to Participate: The Forty Million Dollar Slave

On and off the court, how Black athletes style their hair continues to be a cultural site of struggle and self-determination. Serena Williams, Simone Biles, and Sha'Carri Richardson are just a few of the world-class athletes pushing back on the Eurocentric norms by competing and winning with their hair in a myriad of styles, colors, and textures. These sports—tennis, gymnastics, and track and field—have traditionally restricted access to Black women, and are now experiencing the natural beauty and athletic genius of these women. Similarly, the policing of hair and bodies has long been experienced by many male athletes. Allen Iverson, one of the NBA's former premier shooting guards, was a basketball icon. He openly embraced his roots and connection to hip hop culture and, as a result, was rejected by white society and media. He embraced a streetwear aesthetic that included cornrows, tattoos, and oversized clothing, all while redefining the game of basketball. Despite becoming a multimillionaire, because he did not subscribe to the middle-class Black respectability politics, he was denounced and criticized by Black and white people alike.

Globally, by insisting that Black athletes conform to white standards and comfort, settlers are asking them to abandon themselves and who they are. In a poignant *Players' Tribune* essay about his life as a misunderstood cultural icon and athlete, Iverson shares a seemingly unimportant detail about his passions outside of basketball—he loves to draw. With this small detail he is telling us so much. That he is human, that he is not what we expect or what we've stereotyped him to be based on his appearance, and very importantly, that he is a creator. How we curate our appearance—whether with cornrows, tattoos, fitteds, or diamond jewelry—is a visual art, much like drawing. I often wonder about the many "high-performing" Black people who abandon their interests to pursue money or prestige. Iverson's courage to just be and design himself for himself is the kind of embodied natural resistance that Nikki Giovanni invites us to explore.

In the United States and many parts of Europe, sports were introduced to enslaved peoples as a diversion designed to suppress resistance and revolution. In William C. Rhoden's *Forty Million Dollar Slaves*, he describes the journey from literal plantations to today's figurative ones, in the form of collegiate and professional sports programs. Rhoden specifically highlights that the journey from inner cities or small towns to large athletic programs is one designed to disconnect athletes from their roots and create the conditions for hyper-exploitation by teams, agents, and the media. Though designed for dehumanization, professional sports have become a hotbed for various resistance efforts.

Refusing to participate in a ceremony to pledge allegiance to a country that has violently denied rights to Black people or boycotting dehumanizing interactions is a particularly powerful form of resistance employed by athletes. Take, for example, the lives of athletes Eroseanna "Rose" Robinson and Marshawn Lynch. Long before NFL star quarterback Colin Kaepernick took a knee to protest police brutality, before championship-winning NBA point guard and dashiki wearing Craig Hodges hand-delivered a passionate letter on behalf of poor Black people to George W. Bush, before point guard Mahmoud Abdul-Rauf refused to stand for the flag because of its opposition to his Muslim faith, and before track runners Tommie Smith and John Carlos raised their fists in protest at the 1968 Olympics, a Black woman athlete protested the hypocrisy, injustice, and violence that the American flag represented for Black people—high jumper Rose Robinson.

In the 1959 Pan-American Games, Robinson was the first person in US history to refuse to stand for the national anthem citing that she would not stand for a country that is hypocritical and racist. As a result of her refusal, she was labeled a radical and became a target of the US government. She was jailed for tax evasion because she refused to pay taxes to a bellicose government, and she continued her activist resistance in jail with a hunger strike. The media at the time widely covered this story of tax evasion and her subsequent hunger strike but predictably erased her from history. But we will not forget her—from her antiwar efforts to her principled activism to respond and resist oppression of Black people, she paved the way for other athletes to manifest their values on and off the field.

On the other hand, American football running back Marshawn Lynch demonstrates a different kind of resistance—the Black athlete's direct insubordination. On top of the physical, mental, and emotional labor of careers as professional athletes, high-profile players like Lynch are expected to respond to media obligations or get fined. Players generally regard their contractual press obligations as hostile and routinely dehumanizing interactions. Lynch, a Superbowl champion who is well known for his carefree spirit and creativity on and off the field, began to resist his mandatory press engagements by offering repeatedly uninformative answers. He offered responses like "I'm thankful" and "I'm just here so I won't get fined, bro" to resist and stonewall hungry reporters while evading heavy fines. He insisted on controlling his own narrative by not offering one either with his silence or by providing uninformative responses. We assume that the oppressed always want to be heard, but Lynch demonstrates that there is something very powerful and freeing about being silent or uncooperative.

And sometimes resistance is led by someone on the sideline. Allen Iverson recounts one of his first games as a college basketball player at Georgetown in his *Players' Tribune* essay:

> There were four men, making some noise way up in the stands. And they all had on handcuffs . . . and chains . . . and orange jumpsuits. Those kinds of orange jumpsuits. And I remember the sign they were holding up—clear as day. It said: ALLEN IVERSON: THE NEXT MJ. But then it had "MJ" crossed out. And they had markered in "OJ." . . . Here's what Coach Thompson, MY coach, did for me on that night. . . . he calmly walked over to us, player by player, and told us that—don't worry about our things—we were leaving the floor.
>
> That's it: We were leaving the floor. No big drama. Heads held high. We were there . . . and then we were gone.
>
> And then once we were off that floor, and it was just Coach back on the court. He calmly told those refs, he said, "Hey, no disrespect. No disrespect to y'all. But here's what's going to happen: If you don't get those four pieces of sh*t outta here, and I'm talking immediately—we're gonna be forfeiting this game. Understood?"
>
> They understood, man.

I know this next story through the experience of my neighbor, friend, and former professional Australian football player, Héritier Lumumba. Lumumba spent his time in the Australian Football League as an anomaly; he was among the first players of African descent in the history of the sport. During his tenure as a prominent player for the Collingwood Football Club, he was subjected to horrific indignities on and off the field. He shared his experiences with the club and the league, only to be met with racial gaslighting as they dismissed his experiences, denied acknowledgment, and shaped a public narrative regarding his mental health. He subsequently took legal action and launched a highly successful nationwide public relations campaign that led to a historic reckoning within the nation. The end result was a reorganization of the Collingwood Football Club's leadership, which included the departure of several key figures, including the organization's president, head coach, and other executive members. Additionally, multiple players, including those from other teams, brought their experiences to the public to demand justice and change from the league and the nation's culture of racism.

After leaving Australia shortly after his career ended, Lumumba worked within a global coalition of Indigenous people to build international alliances and connections with individuals, communities, and organizations, reclaiming power and land, and fighting for justice. From learning Indigenous practices to resisting ongoing colonial constructs in professional sports, he is working within a movement for oppressed peoples globally.

In my conversations with Lumumba, he is sure to regularly remind me that before we consider the role sports play in resistance, we must begin with the land where games and entertainment take place—the soil, dirt, grass, and asphalt that are the foundation for almost all sporting activities. One place where the land is especially sacred is in Emeryville, California, a small city in the San Francisco Bay Area. Emeryville was settled on a sacred shellmound burial site of the Ohlone people. For the Ohlone people, like for the people of many Indigenous cultures, burials have great cultural significance in that they establish genealogies and territory. This sanctity has not been respected or maintained; in fact, over the last seventy-five years there has been prolific real estate development on this land. From malls to condos, this sacred land has, and continues to be, gentrified and desecrated.

Ironically, Emeryville is also home to many athletic fields and is mere miles away from the Oakland A's baseball stadium. Not only are athletes, professional and recreational, playing on stolen land, this particular land continues to get pillaged for resources as these sporting groups make millions (sometimes billions) of dollars, all while gentrification accelerates the theft and displacement of the few Indigenous and Black people in the area. This phenomenon of playing on stolen land is not unique to the US; from Australia to South America this pattern continues. Often coinciding with the land theft is a cultural appropriation of sacred Indigenous personhood. In Europe and around the world, many athletic teams exploit Indigenous heritage for names and mascots for teams, but despite the dehumanizing portrayals, African and Indigenous peoples continue to resist.

RESISTANCE IN CAPTIVITY

Europeans locked up Native people in military forts, missions, reservations, boarding schools, and today, increasingly, in state and federal prisons. For American Indians, incarceration is an extension of the history and violent mechanisms of colonization.
—STORMY OGDEN, writer and community organizer

Naybahood Nip, also known as Nipsey Hussle, always felt like a famous cousin to me. He was an Eritrean American who, like me, lived between two worlds: the cultural expectations of the Habesha community and those of the United States. I met and spoke to him once at Merkato on Fairfax. He was with his daughter finishing a meal and I was coming to greet my auntie who owns the restaurant. In that brief interaction I saw a dedicated father offer *gorshas* to his daughter while intently paying attention to her every word between bites. He appeared to be a regular as he greeted the waitresses and shopped with familiarity in the grocery section of the restaurant. On his way out, in typical and traditional Habesha style, he bowed and said goodbye to everyone in the restaurant.

Although this brief encounter demonstrates a great deal about the kind of man Nipsey was, he was also a loving partner, a famous rapper, a former member of the Rollin' 60s, a businessman, and an all-around hood hero. His life's work, personal and professional, was to unlock and release the potential of those held in captivity. He knew first-hand what it meant to grow up and live in oppression, both in South LA and Asmara. His art reflected his experience and his self-education. In his song "Dedication," he understands the power of his message and invites us to "swim against" the waves—in other words, resist the heavy current of the status quo. This song is emblematic of the many songs he wrote before his untimely death in 2019; he wrote it for his family, friends, neighbors, and, most importantly, himself. With long braided hair, face tattoos, and his own distinct fashion (and clothing brand), he was frequently misrecognized and misrepresented as a violent gang member by most people.

Scholar and writer Imani Perry discusses the role of hip hop and its deliberate physical and metaphorical opposition to mainstream settler cultural norms in her book *Prophets of the Hood: Politics and Poetics in Hip Hop*. Hip hop, in many ways, is inherently defined by resistance as the genre embraces the outlaw and those at the margins. Still, there is a deeper meaning of this positionality. Perry writes that being an outlaw, "on a deeper, more symbolic level, . . . is achieved through a position of resistance to the confines of status quo existence." She suggests that outlaws, or outlaw values, are a resistance to the norms that unfairly punish Black people or discount their choices. This perspective itself kind of creates an alternative set of values, norms, and ideals that oppose the settler norm.

Those who are caged, literally and figuratively, are held captive, not just by their built environment, but by a system designed to deny and erase their humanity. From Central California Women's Facility to the public housing complex of Nickerson Gardens, the settler logic of brutality, dehumanization, disposability, and invisibility continues to harm those inside and outside the walls of those institutions. In a literal sense, prisons, penitentiaries, or other settler colonial institutions like residential schools are vestiges of settler colonialism's violent past. Take for instance, mass incarceration, which exists and is reproduced in a historical context that dates back to the chattel enslavement of African people worldwide, or how the material conditions and environment in US prisons are not markedly different from the so-called missionary schools for African children or residential schools for Native Americans.

Stormy Ogden, a Pomo woman, researcher, and former prisoner, experienced this connection first hand. She has been outspoken about the many ways the Native American people have been incarcerated in different forms of penitentiaries since the arrival of the settler. To that end, in a contribution to the book *Neo-Colonial Injustice and the Mass Imprisonment of Indigenous Women,* Ogden aptly observes, "As the bible and bottle were used to gain control over Indian lands and deny Native sovereignty, prisons—in one form or another—have been used to control Indian bodies. Prisons are instruments of racism and social control, constructed by a system whose purpose is to isolate and dehumanize." Ogden's critical connection between well-intentioned approaches like the bible, and more addictive ones like alcohol, demonstrates the direct assault to Native bodies and spirits. Whether backed by good intentions or not, the purpose and design of settler incarceration was, and continues to be, to dominate and subjugate Native peoples.

Contrary to what appears in American textbooks, enslaved Africans of the Americas did not accept their kidnapping and enslavement without resistance. Whether born into enslavement or captured, they resisted in a variety of ways to secure freedom and express their own humanity. Their resistance manifested in the oppressed finding ways to control their own minds and bodies. This took the form of hunger strikes onboard slave ships or breaking plantation tools to protest the long and unpaid labor of enslavement.

Another important way some enslaved people protested their situation was by running away; some left and disappeared into local Native American communities while others joined maroon societies. In light of the brutal historical context of settler colonialism, many people assume resistance by the oppressed was necessarily violent. Settler colonial responses to conditions of neglect, hardship, and deprivation have historically resulted in violence and retaliation. The settler logic, therefore, projects its own behavior onto the oppressed and denies any other definition of resistance that is not defined by cruelty and brutality. But resistance can mean so much more.

Resistance has the capacity to produce structural change if it is intentional, disciplined, and principled.

Recently, the Covid-19 virus exposed the value settlers' have for the vulnerable. Around the world, we witnessed how those in prisons and those without homes were placed at highest risk for contracting and dying from the virus. Functionally, these spaces provided inadequate ways to social distance, or test, track, and treat people. Covid-19 exposed an international crisis that highlighted a chronically poor healthcare infrastructure for those living outside as well as those living in prisons. This crisis, coupled with the prevailing belief that those who are incarcerated and unhoused are disposable and invisible, proved to be deadly. By design and function, prisons, hospitals, schools, and many other institutions (intentionally or unintentionally) participate in the ongoing violence of settler colonialism by creating cycles of neglect and denial of shelter, care, or dignity.

Dinos Christianopoulos remind us that despite settlers' best efforts to bury us, "they do not know we are seeds." Many of the most innovative and inspirational feats of resistance have occurred in captivity. We see people captive in prisons and neglected neighborhoods resist their conditions and re-create themselves and their world, first by fortifying their self-determination and then by clarifying their vision for the world. Black, African, and Native peoples have resisted and continue to resist carceral colonialism through recalling the past, preserving their respective cultures, and political activism. The lives of Stormy Ogden, Huey P. Newton, Angela Y. Davis, El-Hajj Malik el-Shabazz, Winnie Mandela, George Jackson, Ericka Huggins, Leonard Peltier, and countless other brilliant thinkers and social designers have been held captive; some have even been sentenced to solitary confinement or sentenced to death. Even Jesus Christ was a prisoner and held captive before his ultimate state-sanctioned execution. Not submitting to societal judgment and violence and instead maintaining one's humanity is a kind of righteous resistance that can transform the world as we know it.

Some might confuse or romanticize time spent in confinement or captivity as a time to think or fundamentally reform. Though reform and

transformation can happen in these spaces, it is in spite of the harsh conditions, certainly not because of them.

Just because a rose can grow from concrete does not mean concrete is
fertile ground for rose bushes. We can appreciate the genius and struggle
of the many incarcerated and formerly incarcerated people and simultaneously underscore the immeasurable emotional, psychological, physical, and
spiritual hardship they endured to resist their environment and learn, teach,
and think in spite of it all.

In many design circles, the conversation to ameliorate the chronic and
deadly conditions in prisons has largely been focused on the ways to redesign or reform the prison facility or the built environment itself. Frank
Gehry, a well-known, white, Canadian architect and designer of several
concert halls and museums, has never designed a prison or worked deeply
with the community on the impacts of incarceration. He did, however,
spend one night in jail for possession of marijuana. According to *Architectural Digest*, he was so moved by his one-night experience behind bars, that
he left determined to reform the space. He went on to teach a class at Yale
in 2017 on this very theme of designing better prisons and became the
focus of a documentary on the same topic called *Frank Gehry: Building Justice*.
In the documentary he asks, "What if we start treating people like human
beings—what would prison look like?" This well-intentioned question tells
us so much about the many limitations of white designers designing based
on cursory observations.

Rather than considering how to redesign our world and society to
eliminate the conditions that create carcerality, state-sanctioned violence,
and policies that disproportionality lock up Black and Indigenous peoples,
the designer's response is to create prisons fit for humans. In other words,
dorm rooms rather than cells for prisoners. This approach is surprising
because architecture as a discipline requires incredible due diligence and
exploration of projects before any design takes place. The best architects
use their senses, intuition, and imagination to create spaces that allow
people to be free.

Despite the aspirations of architecture, it is still polluted by settler social
systems. Is it a coincidence that Gehry, a white man who benefits from

settler colonialism, thought that he would be well positioned to teach on the topic of prison facility redesign? Why did *Architectural Digest* report on this story as an altruistic endeavor? How is the media complicit in amplifying and promoting reform propaganda? Why were the models Gehry proposed based on Scandinavian prison design? Why weren't African or other Indigenous approaches to address harm and safety explored? These questions and many others expose the limitations of dominant designer motivations.

Those on the outside of institutions of captivity have much to learn about resistance, particularly from those who are or have been held captive. Resistance, for those of us who are more free, calls us to ask questions of ourselves. Questions like these: What do I think I know and what are the sources for that knowledge? Are those sources reliable? Are there alternatives to what I think? Without questioning ourselves and the structures designed to reproduce settler logics, we run the risk of designing out of hubris or conceit, not care or urgency. It's not enough to observe and experience; we must explore root causes and sit in the discomfort that we benefit from settler designed systems and society.

Typically, the practice of questioning to understand the root causes lead us to radical ideas. For instance, if every person lived in a community where they were housed, ate fresh foods, had access to childcare, quality healthcare, excellent schools, worked a job they enjoyed that paid well, and had good relationships with their neighbors, that community would likely experience little crime. In that community, there would be no need for a massive prison facility since the vast majority of people would be healthy and cared for where they live. It would not be absurd or impossible to imagine such a community without a prison.

For many people, it is easier to accept the institution of prison rather than interrogate the designed conditions of poverty and violence that sustain them. Not having a place where we relegate people who make mistakes and harm others is not only unimaginable, it's scary. Less explored are what conditions and circumstances were designed to lead to incarceration. Is incarceration effective? Are we safer and is harm reduced as a result of incarceration? Are the laws themselves racist, is there racist enforcement of the law, or is it both? Are violations of the law a function and result of extreme poverty, neglect, and deprivation? How do we know someone is guilty with certainty? Or, most critically, why do we think a "justice" system that has repeatedly failed Black and Indigenous people should only be incrementally changed?

In any community, when we lose a person to incarceration or other captivity, we lose important cultural and familial brilliance and brightness. Although some of us interrogate a system designed to reduce the humanity, power, and potential of the oppressed, we must also build relationships, study, and struggle with Black and Indigenous people with lived experience to design new ways of being and doing.

Connecting with the past and knowing ourselves allows us to assert and stand up for our individual and collective humanity.

What if we saw the true value of the discarded, the invisible, and the captive? What if we reconsidered and resisted stereotypes and assumptions about Black people, particularly those in captivity? No matter how small the resistance may seem, it is our opportunity to demonstrate agency and claim control over our own time, labor, and, ultimately, existence.

RAGE AND RESISTANCE

Settler colonial norms dictate that anger is a negative and unproductive emotion. This belief nicely complements the subversive and subtle ways settler societies sow the seeds of docility and assimilation in the oppressed. Anger and rage are not the same. Over time, the past has shown us how Black and Indigenous anger is routinely met with severe consequences—prison or death. It is critical to distinguish between the anger and rage of Black women and that of the self-righteous white men. Take for example, the white man who murdered a group of elders at Bible study at Emanuel African Methodist Episcopal Church in Charleston, South Carolina—indeed, he was angry. We see here that anger can be deadly and disastrous if shaped by violence and white supremacy. We must understand anger not in terms of what is demonstrated by white supremacists and settlers but on the terms of Black feminists like Audre Lorde. Anger is a form of grief. Lorde's reframing of anger is critical to distinguishing the role of anger and rage for the Black woman. In her 1981 keynote "The Uses of Anger" at the National Women's Studies Association Conference in Storrs, Connecticut, she says:

> Women responding to racism means women responding to anger; Anger of exclusion, of unquestioned privilege, of racial distortions, of silence, ill-use, stereotyping, defensiveness, misnaming, betrayal, and co-optation.

> But anger expressed and translated into action in the service of our vision and our future is a liberating and strengthening act of clarification, for it is in the painful process of this translation that we identify who are our allies with whom we have grave differences, and who are our genuine enemies.

Lorde talks about how rage within progressive settings is not theoretical but very personal. She offers two particularly personal examples that resonate deeply with me. In a professional context, she recalls her experience at an academic conference speaking on anger, and a white woman says to her, "Tell me how you feel but don't say it too harshly or I cannot hear you." This response elucidates the desire of white women to be centered at the expense of the Black woman's pain by not engaging with the message, a message that may change the white woman's way of life. Lorde goes on to explore rage in an everyday context with one of her most precious relationships, that of her child. She recounts,

> I wheel my two-year-old daughter in a shopping cart through a super-market in Eastchester in 1967, and a little white girl riding past in her mother's cart calls out excitedly, "Oh look, Mommy, a baby maid!" And your mother shushes you, but she does not correct you. And so, fifteen years later, at a conference on racism, you can still find that story humorous. But I hear your laughter is full of terror and disease.

Anger and rage offer us a connection to our humanity that is not tethered to the comfort of whiteness or settler logic, which makes it virtuous and productive. Anger is a natural response and consequence of ongoing settler colonization. Rage, in particular, expressed in disciplined ways, offers us new worlds. Rather than taking responsibility for the past and present conditions of settler colonization, settlers shame and stigmatize Black and Indigenous anger while condoning and pathologizing the anger of white people.

After a conversation with Buddhist leader Thich Nhat Hanh, bell hooks spoke of the importance of anger. She offered the analogy of fertilizing a garden with compost: "hold on to your anger, and use it as compost for your garden . . . if we think of anger as compost . . . as energy that can be recycled in the direction of our good, it is an empowering force. If we don't think about it that way, it becomes a debilitating and destructive force." Expressing and embracing anger and rage, a rational and human response to extreme oppression, can be cathartic and nourishing to ourselves and society.

In many faith-based community organizing practices, anger is described as temperature, on a spectrum of hot to cold. Hot anger usually incites the individual to act whereas cold anger is more calculated. Mary Beth Rogers, author of *Cold Anger: A Story of Faith and Power Politics* explains the role of anger. She points out that cold anger "is an anger that seethes at the injustices of life and transforms itself into a compassion for those hurt by life. It is an anger rooted in direct experience and held in collective memory. It is the kind of anger that can energize a democracy—because it can lead to the first step in changing politics." This understanding of anger highlights the nuanced way anger can affirm the dignity of those oppressed, provide hope, and build deep relationships through engaging collective memory and imagining new possibilities. In some ways this emphasis, on alternative ways of being, like those that embrace anger, contradicts traditional settler design.

Take, for instance, formally trained design practitioners. They are encouraged to create delight (as defined by their own standards) and eliminate discomfort or friction for the "user." And yet designing in this way can produce a kind of toxic positivity that manifests as extreme aversion to negativity, anger, discomfort, or distressing information rather than an opportunity to acknowledge and embrace the transformation anger can produce. Too often, an exaggerated focus on the positive in the settler context results in a denial and intentional neglect of the brutal and violent realities of the oppressed. To design and create for Black freedom and joy requires us to embrace the complexity of anger and harness it to catalyze innovation.

BLACK JOY AS RESISTANCE

Resistance is the secret of joy.

—ALICE WALKER, novelist, poet, and activist; in *Possessing the Secret of Joy*

Joy is the unequivocal certainty of one's own humanity and celebration of it—and this is an act of resistance. A sense of self that can't be commodified or colonized. In her poem "won't you celebrate with me," lucille clifton reminds Black women of their humanity when she invites the reader to celebrate with her because she is still alive despite the daily attempts by the world to kill her. The project of self-determination, freedom, and ultimately, worldbuilding, is one Black people around the world have historically led and currently lead. Griot and writer Tracey Michae'l Lewis-Giggetts talks of the ever-present and often-hidden experience of *Black joy*, living and loving loud in the face of oppression. She asserts that joy definitely can have a race, and that Black joy is uniquely rooted in our ancestral expressions of Blackness across the diaspora. This experience is especially important for Black women as we continue to carry the burden of invisibility and hyper-exploitation. From the way we style our hair, to the distinct way we dance, dress, sing, joke, and express our sexuality—even our body-unique physical features—all are dehumanized and strangely duplicated by non-Black people.

The radicality and hard-fought nature of Black joy is precisely what excludes non-Black people from appropriating it. Cultural appropriation and, even in some cases, appreciation attempt to access this mysterious expression of joy. To be clear, (Black) joy and happiness are not the same. The difference is, as my elders say, that "joy can't nobody take from you" and happiness is a feeling of being pleased that is momentary or temporary. Our efforts to design a better world should generate joy, learning, and pleasure. Pleasure and danger, together, can transform ideas and people and, in that process, we can invent ourselves and our world.

Resistance should facilitate a restful return to ourselves, our true selves. Selves that are whole and healed, that are free from trauma, hardship, and despair, and in some cases, selves we have not yet experienced.

RESISTANCE AS INVISIBLE, IMAGINATIVE, AND INSURGENT

It is better to be invisible.
—BEN OKRI, poet and novelist, in *Astonishing the Gods*

The spirit world, our inner selves, our beliefs—these are the forces that motivate all that we do. Some of the most important parts of our lives are unseen. Our beliefs, ideas, faith, discovery, and power are realized and exercised within ourselves, and they are usually not obvious to the outside world. We must remind ourselves that the unseen things are usually the most valuable and the seen things are their byproducts. Take for instance, the experience of *metanoia*—a kind of whole-being conversion that compels change and self-correction. People experience metanoia when they decide for themselves to pursue their full potential and abandon their old ways. When someone leaves an abusive relationship, commits to a movement, renounces their participation in a cult, or confesses to a crime, it is usually a result of experiencing metanoia.

Every day, in every choice, we make conscious and unconscious decisions about what we will accept as individuals and communities. Individually and independently Black people have resisted the oppressive hand of settler colonial power. The threat of state violence has been both real and invisible, as has the chronic degradation of the environment. These invisible settler and capitalistic forces have always been met with defense and resistance.

Harriet Tubman experienced metanoia. Often referred to as Black Moses, Tubman freed nearly eight hundred enslaved Black women, men, and children. As an enslaved person who would not accept enslavement, she often experienced violence at the hand of slaveholders. However, that never stopped her from dreaming. In fact, one serious head injury she sustained while intervening in the abuse of another enslaved person caused her to slip into trances and have visions that accessed her superpowers. Tubman had a spiritual and transformative relationship to dreaming that translated to her waking demand of freedom. She regularly declared, "My People Are

Free!" The present tense of her statement was a testament to her faith in her dream. The invisible and intuitive force that guided her to and through her oppression is one to inspire all of us. Black women, in the US and abroad, represent a long genealogy of insurgency and activism toward the fight for freedom dreams. Harriet Tubman's life and legacy are a testament to this embodied freedom.

Insurgent spaces, not to be confused with Black replicas of colonial spaces, intentionally disagree with the formal and informal laws and expectation of predesigned spaces. We create those spaces with the caveat that some institutions cannot be "decolonized" or "reimagined" out of their primary function—the maintenance of social/racial/gendered/abled/economic oppression. Our energy is best spent resisting this status quo and exploring self-discovery, danger, and pleasure.

The objective of resistance is to be free in an unfree environment. Free from violence, harm, and oppression, able to disentangle ourselves from the obsession and hoarding of our visible things, instead being known by the things that are not material, physical, or tangible. While this might seem impossible or implausible, working to achieve this is the difficult path to building a regenerative world. Evading, ignoring, rebelling, and otherwise thwarting the reach of the settler allows Black people to move beyond waiting for the moral conscience of the powerful to dictate and determine their own fate. Oppressed people are more than victims of the oppression they experience. We are emancipators and fighters who have created and continue to create legacies that benefit all of us, even the settler.

In the end, I submit that the theory and practice of resistance is internal, insurgent, and invisible. We are called to be fugitives and traitors to the settler colonial way of life that includes borders, race, and other oppressive structures. *Fugitivity*, one's ability to escape danger and find respite, is the precondition to metanoia and long-term transformation. Tubman's fugitivity was a struggle for the transformation from enslaved to free that seemed impossible at the time but ultimately inspired people (and still inspires people) for the generations that followed. Fugitive practices of survival and resistance in the face of oppression and exploitation refuse to acknowledge borders—those borders between people and places. The borders that condemn some, namely Black people, as nonhuman and denote others as human. Through deliberation, design, and the divine, fugitive resistance offers us the power to dream and act, to engage prophetic visioning—all in service of ending the world as we know it and creating a world worthy of the brilliance and brightness of Black people worldwide.

DESIGNING THE GREAT TABLE

Too many people are fighting for a seat at a table that Jesus would have flipped.

—PASTOR MICHAEL MCBRIDE OF THE WAY CHRISTIAN CENTER IN BERKELEY, California

Most of our built environments are designed. From the roads we travel, to the food we consume, to what we wear and how we wear it—even our recreational activities are products of our own or someone else's imagination. Dreaming and designing are both Indigenous and integral to oppressed people's survival and thriving. For some, having a seat at an existing table is sufficient to design, free of systems of oppression; for many others, a seat at a table designed for and by settlers to maintain settler power cannot be used.

Recalling "The Parable of the Table" at the start of this section, we see the metaphor of a seat at the table is one we can continue to extend and explore with new practical and philosophical questions. For instance:

- Why do I need a table?
- What purpose does a table serve?
- What do tables represent in my culture? Does that contradict other uses or cultural contexts?
- What does this table suggest about my beliefs?
- Do I want a seat at a table that denied my mother a seat?
- What makes a table worthy of joining?
- How was the table made? Who made it? How were the materials and labor sourced?

- Is the table environmentally sustainable?
- Is the table broken beyond repair?
- Is the table designed only for able-bodied people?
- What would a table look like if I created it?
- Can I design a different way to connect with others that doesn't require a table or seat or other props?
- What are other ways people gather?

My own responses to these questions suggest that the table itself is a manifestation of exploitation, exclusion, and burden. I believe that some things can't be repaired. Lorde famously professes that "The master's tools will never dismantle the master's house," and while this adage suggests that we find new ways to repair what is flawed or broken, I respectfully disagree with the premise of the quote. That is to say, I am not interested in the burden of fixing or redesigning the master's house, nor do I want to concern myself with a structure that, from its very foundation, was built on enslavement, genocide, and ongoing exploitation. I am not interested in redesigning or reforming the establishment. It is not in my nature or my spirit to join a fundamentally flawed system. The expected labor of the oppressed, to not only recall the terror and trauma of our experiences but to then continue to operate in a structure or system with minor (and usually cosmetic) changes, will not produce the world that embraces our humanity and offers real justice. Simply put, I don't want a seat at the colonizers' table, and I don't want to renovate their house.

DESIGNING FOR F(R)ICTION

People who say change is impossible are usually pretty happy with things just as they are.
—N. K. JEMISIN, science fiction writer, *The City We Became*

Just as sound requires the friction between two elements (a bow on a string, a hammer on a piano wire, air through vocal cords), so too do we need

friction between different ways of being, such as where two or more traditions collide. Here the metaphor of friction illustrates the necessity of
resistance to create something new and unique to both elements, something
that is not reducible to the sum of those parts. Friction is a fruitful way to
decolonize because it focuses attention to the desires and experiences of
the oppressed and colonized. By producing friction, we send a message to
the settler project that oppressed peoples will not be assimilated or extin-
guished. Ultimately, this is the work of reimagining and designing a world
that can be informed by both Indigenous tradition and future orientations
that move away from settler colonization.

One way the oppressed can design their own worlds full of potential
and freedom is by participating in the inventive and imaginative world of
creating fiction. The oppression of Black and other Indigenous people is
predicated on creating a world of friction and hardship, one where we may
not see a way outside of that reality. Afrofuturism is one way friction and
fiction come together to imagine and design a better future. *Afrofuturism* is a
cultural aesthetic that combines science fiction, alternative history, and fan-
tasy to explore the Black experience. Coined by author Mark Dery in the
1994 essay "Black to the Future," Afrofuturism names speculative fiction
within the African diaspora. Afrofuturist writers like N. K. Jemisin, artists
like Jean-Michel Basquiat, and musicians like Sun Ra and George Clinton
have produced works that examine narratives and ways of being to design
living outside of the dominant cultural narrative.

Octavia E. Butler, a prophetic and prolific Black science fiction writer
to which this book is forever indebted, showed her readers that fiction has
a ruthless logic to its design. Through her books and ideas, she explores the
network and constellation of power and affection in human relationships.
In Butler's 1979 novel *Kindred*, she tells the story of time travel through narratives of enslaved peoples and science fiction. In writing the story, Butler
designed her own underground railroad between past and present so that
the aperture of the reader's imagination could be dramatically widened.
Butler's work was visionary and offered people like me a path from which
to access our own power to create an alternative future. Like most Black
women, nonbinary, and queer writers, Butler challenged gender norms in

her genre and anti-Blackness in her narratives but also in her profession. Her work, and her very being, continues to transform science fiction and the world.

We all have a role to play in designing and imagining a future where we all prosper. By designing resistance, we are actively participating in that transformation. For some, incremental change is tolerable, but transformation is too disruptive to life as they know it. Others find that the status quo of settler colonialism works very well for them and offers them power and privilege that they'd rather not lose. For those most oppressed, the only way to a dignified existence is through self-definition, transformation, and creation.

To begin that process, I submit that we answer these questions:

- What is the role and purpose of design for you and your kin?
- Why do we design?
- Who are we when we design?

My answers to these questions are ever evolving. Today, as I write this book, I believe design is theory and action, together: theory that recalls the status quo and focuses on imagination. I design because I must survive empire. However I create because it is my inheritance and because my loved ones' well-being depends on it.

When I design, I produce the fertile ground to create and grow new life. The conception and birthing process cannot happen alone. Design is important, and yet, it is not the central way to create freedom. Studying and struggling in community is how I engage my radical imagination. I offer this as one way to consider design practices that reflect who I am and where I came from. The answers to these questions need not be as direct as mine; in fact, often the answers are more nuanced.

For instance, I recently visited the Baldwin Hills Crenshaw Farmers Market in Los Angeles, where I was introduced to the analogy of creation and design being similar to cooking. My neighbor, and our resident hood philosopher, explained to a small crowd of us strawberry-sampling women, that everyone can create or design—some people go to school to specialize, some have hours of practice, some are naturally gifted, and others design for basic survival, but all of us can and do design/create/cook. This analogy of

cooking deeply resonated with the crowd because although eating is something we all do, the process of cooking is not the same for everyone. Some
people are vegan, whereas others eat whatever is available. Some people
are retired and can spend hours prepping and cooking, while others eat in
the car on the go. Extending the analogy even further, cooking/eating and
fasting/not eating are ways people create their existence. For many African
cultures, like Ethiopian, people fast as a way to connect with the divine and
create blessed communities. So, both the presence and absence of food can
facilitate one's design faculties. The serendipitous farmers market interaction left much food for thought, most notably, that design and creation are
accessible to us all.

In many parts of the world, designs are created or coopted by dominant groups, namely white settlers. In Part I, we explored the deliberate displacement, exploitation, and erasure of African and Indigenous languages,
lands, and lifestyles. Let us revisit, differently, that which settler colonialism
has imposed on exploited people and how they remembered and resisted
(and continue to resist) to maintain and assert their humanity. Designing,
with the primary goal of resistance, requires us to consider first what consti-
tutes a safe and sacred space to be ourselves.

How we create spaces, things, systems, places—all are a manifestation of our beliefs. Where we put freeways and factories may seem to be
because we designed purely for terrain and geography, but there is no such
thing as neutral design. How we design and plan cities has downstream
consequences that result in unclean water, extreme air pollution, and other
markers of environmental racism and harm to poor and unhoused people.
Meanwhile in white, wealthier neighborhoods these issues don't exist.
These communities are designed with lots of green space, clean air and
water, plenty of fresh food options, and they have responsive systems when
issues arise. It is not a coincidence that Black and Indigenous peoples are
trapped in housing projects and on reservations while white people live in
safer, cleaner communities—that is by design.

Design industries are in decay and decline. While economically profit-
able, many design firms and popular design approaches represent a kind of
intellectually lazy attempt to create in a human-centered way. The design

industry has been complicit in creating compliance and suppressing resistance. Too often, we see design practitioners rely on status quo methods with minor and performative changes rather than grasping at the root. Tactics like adding empathy to an already extractive design thinking process or creating checklists of tasks or other shortcuts to avoid bias—all result in mechanical, cold, and fundamentally superficial prototypes and outcomes that can be performative and sometimes harmful to minoritized groups.

For instance, a designer creating a new program or product for an oppressed person might first try to empathize with that person. Some common ways of empathizing include taking the time to understand the person by trying to build a quick relationship, exploring the world as they would in a "day in the life of" exercise, or worse, trying to walk in someone else's proverbial shoes. There are several issues with this approach. First, quick relationships are typically transactional and often leave the "user" feeling exploited and used. Second, pretending to mimic someone else's day means you have to assume a lot about the way they live and how they experience the world. Finally, anytime you ask someone if you can walk in their shoes, you are asking for their shoes, and often it's the shoes they have on. In other words, you are asking a great deal of a person who you don't have a real relationship with, and in many settings and cultures, that is offensive. Empathy, though well intentioned, can be harmful and can turn ruinous if you don't have a real relationship and self-awareness.

As designers and people who experience design, we must be more concerned with the process than the prototype. Resistance in design can be as straightforward as refusing to engage in ethnographic research, or it can be more nuanced, as in resisting the many ways design has perpetuated the myth of the individual and scarcity, or how it has coopted and corrupted other approaches to creating, being, and doing. No matter what form of resistance you choose, the survival and joy of oppressed peoples are connected to our collective ability to define ourselves for ourselves, as ancestor and feminist scholar Audre Lorde reminds us. In spite of extreme violence and exploitation, the oppressed still have tremendous cultural inheritance embodied in our lifestyle, land, language, and labor that stop, and begin to reverse, settler colonialism.

Designing resistance slows down systems and calls the powerful (people and institutions) to grapple with the issues of the oppressed. Those who resist are making demands while maintaining their sense of self, and in some cases, they are facilitating the restoration of dignity of the oppressor in allowing them to repair harm. When embraced, the discomfort and tension produced by resistance create the conditions for self-determination and cognitive justice, necessary preconditions for freedom.

DESIGN TO DEFY

You cannot carry out fundamental change without a certain amount of madness. In this case, it comes from nonconformity, the courage to turn your back on the old formulas, the courage to invent the future. It took the madmen of yesterday for us to be able to act with extreme clarity today. I want to be one of those madmen. We must dare to invent the future.
—THOMAS SANKARA, former president of Burkina Faso

Whether it is with landscape architecture or community organizing, the process of remembering and resisting the past and present settler colonial structures and systems is one that unequivocally requires courage. Thomas Sankara, the former president of Burkina Faso, was an anti-imperialist leader who weaved together Pan-Africanism, feminism, food justice, and environmentalism to dream and design a new Burkina Faso free from French colonial influence. Burkina Faso gained its independence when Sankara was eleven years old, but that did not mean the country was free from colonial rule. He observed a persistent phenomenon of settler colonialism across the continent after independence was gained—crippling debt. In a speech he delivered as president at the summit of the Organization of African Unity in Addis Ababa in July of 1987, he explains, "Debt's origins come from colonialism's origins. Those who lend us money are those who colonized us. . . . Under its current form, controlled and dominated by imperialism, debt is a skillfully managed reconquest of Africa, intended to subjugate its growth and development through foreign rules."

Rather than participate in an inherently exploitative relationship that extended an evolved version of colonialism, Sankara refused to pay those debts. He contended that rejecting colonial economic structures and subjectivity was not an "aggressive move" but a "fraternal move" to invite both colonizer and colonized to tell the truth. For Sankara, defying colonial infrastructure included defying the colonial Eurocentric knowledge systems. In his mind, the tendency to pay tribute, subtly or intentionally, or idolize European standards, states, and societies diminishes the ability of the oppressed to pursue self-determination. Being willing to do something that hasn't been done in the name of self-determination requires clarity and courage with which to envision a future dramatically different from the conditions of settler colonialism. Moreover, defiance slows down productivity and thereby slows down the predatory nature of capitalism. Sankara demonstrated how defying settler colonialism meant refusing subjugation and violence in its many forms and iterations. He continued to demonstrate the courage to defy colonial rule by renaming the country. Its colonial name was Upper Volta, but he changed that to Burkina Faso, which draws from two native languages and means "the land of upright men" or "men of integrity."

As president, Sankara was wildly popular with the people. He worked with communities to create collectivist policies to make the nation self-sufficient. Unfortunately, despite designing revolutionary new policies and earning grassroot support, he had a target on his back painted there by colonial entities. After only five years of governing, he and a few of his colleagues were assassinated outside a government building. Although many believe the French government was behind the assassination, the case is still open.

It is ironic that defiance has the stigma of suggesting violence, hostility, or confrontation for disobeying conventional institutional settler rules, sensibilities, and ultimately, lifestyle. Yet, those who stand up for freedom are often labeled defiant, are met with violence and, in some cases, death. We must remember and recall these valiant people and the lesson that it is the defiant "madmen" who are remembered for their role in transforming our world.

Deliverance for a Defiant People

Denial or dismissal tends to be the first response of the Western scientific and academic community when information is rooted in Black or Indigenous knowledge and is presented without institutional validation. Much like the "discovery" that trees communicate is the "discovery" of the swampland that runaway enslaved peoples inhabited and built communities in that were undetected. The Great Dismal Swamp, which encompasses territory in southeast Virginia and northeast North Carolina, had been considered uninhabitable due to its thick vegetation. Up until recently most American anthropologists, archaeologists, and historians agreed that it was impossible that large groups of people lived in the area. Even more impossible was that this area was previously inhabited by Black Seminoles and other marooners.[*] But in the early 1700s the Great Dismal Swamp was a thriving refuge and it remained that way for more than a century.

Archaeologist Daniel O. Sayers spent years learning about the archaeology of maroons, Indigenous Americans, and escaped enslaved laborers in the Great Dismal Swamp. He led one of the most thorough and unconventional archeological excavations of this unique region. Sayers relied heavily on the narratives and artifacts of these defiant communities that thrived outside of the settler colonial, capitalistic context.

In his book *A Desolate Place for a Defiant People* he discusses the impact and influence of the peoples who "self-extricated" and built literal and figurative new worlds. Sayers exposes and unravels the complex social and economic systems developed by these defiant communities that thrived on the periphery. He develops an analytical framework based on the complex interplay between alienation, diasporic exile, uneven geographical development,

---

[*] Poet and decolonial writer Edouard Glissant offers this definition of marronage, marrons: The *marrons*, "Maroons," are fugitive slaves, and *marronage*, originally the political act of these slaves who escaped into the forested hills of Martinique, now designates a form of cultural opposition to European-American culture. This resistance takes its strength from a combination of geographical connectedness (essential to survival in the jungle and absent in the descendants of slaves alienated from the land that could never be theirs), memory, and all the canny detours, diversions, and ruses required to deflect the repeated attempts to recuperate this cultural subversion.

and modes of production to argue that colonialism and slavery inevitably created sustained critiques of American oppression and exploitation. He writes:

> These people performed a critique of a brutal capitalistic enslavement system, and they rejected it completely. They risked everything to live in a more just and equitable way, and they were successful for ten generations. One of them, a man named Charlie, was interviewed later in Canada. He said that all labor was communal here. That's how it would have been in an African village.

These are especially important revelations that offer us insight into our modern-day settler colonial and enslavement context and the possibilities beyond it. The Black, Indigenous peoples, and marooners who lived in the swamp mostly used ancient native techniques and organic swamp materials that decomposed quickly, which makes it difficult to validate the existence of artifacts using traditional scientific methods.

The limited amount of formal Western documentation and archaeological research has stunted our collective awareness and understanding of the actual social history of the Great Dismal Swamp. Accordingly, our national historical narratives and comprehensions are very much incomplete. Sayers demonstrates that this lack of knowledge is damaging to our collective sense of our national and even world history. Some of the most successful and transformative social radicals of the modern era have gone unnoticed and unrecognized for centuries.

These special people of the Great Dismal Swamp who acted in total defiance for more than a hundred years are among the few who have successfully undercut and escaped the brutal and anti-Black world settlers made for themselves. They were successful because they accurately critiqued the racialized capitalistic settler colonial context within which they were embedded prior to their escape to the swamp. Over the past five centuries the various peoples of the Great Dismal Swamp have been an inspiring and incredible micro-minority whose form of consciousness and resistance to subjugation and exploitation radically transformed the world. It is just that they did it in ways we might not predict or know until we look at the evidence they left behind. Ultimately, the people of the Great Dismal Swamp undermined a brutal and anti-Black society. These runaway enslaved people who escaped the dangerous and violent settler colony created something new, something invisible and out of sight of the settler gaze. They defined resistance and dignity for themselves and intentionally designed a new world with different social, political, and economic rules.

Refuse to Reform: Decolonize Design

Ethiopian Empress Taytu Betul was known by her favorite word *embi*! Loosely translated, *embi* means "hell no." Her emphatic and unequivocal refusal was what kept Ethiopia free from settler colonialism while most of the continent was under European rule. This was in large part because she refused to be a docile and submissive partner to Emperor Menelik II, refused to be out of proximity from ordinary Ethiopians and those on the front lines of battle, and most importantly, refused to compromise with the occupying Italians.

In late 1895, after reading a proposed treaty by the Italians, it became clear to Empress Taytu that the Italian occupation of Ethiopia was not for friendship but for colonization. She informed her husband, the emperor, that the Italians were not only acting in bad faith but attempting to clandestinely colonize the Ethiopians. He insisted that she "calm down" and compromise, as he believed she was overreacting. She refused to be gaslit and accept his assessment. Instead, she confronted the Italians and asked them to leave before the Ethiopian people waged war. Shocked and insulted that a woman had the audacity to speak to them in that way, the Italians doubled down and prepared for battle.

Taytu joined the army as a general near an Italian fort in Makelle. There she saw the staggering number of Italian soldiers and artillery, and she knew the Ethiopians would not be able to defeat them on the battlefield under those conditions. So rather than engaging in a frontal attack, she designed a plan to cut off the Italian water supply, thereby forcing them to retreat to their country. The thirsty Italians were forced to surrender and return home after less than two weeks without water. A month later the war ended with an Ethiopian victory at the Battle of Adwa in 1896.

By leveraging her unique lived experience and geographical knowledge, Empress Taytu led the Ethiopian army to defeat the Italians without guns or physical combat. It is notable that this strategy enlisted the labor of only nine hundred military personnel. In other words, her resistance required the concerted effort of a small group of people to stop a war. As a result of her vision, principles, and strategy, Ethiopia remains one of the few countries in Africa never to be colonized.

I tell this story not to glorify war and military resistance but to highlight our unique knowledges as Africans and Black people and our ability to resist in our own way, rather than matching the violence inflicted on us. Empress Taytu proved to be a brilliant strategist, commander, leader, and partner, all because she refused and resisted traditional cultural norms and the status quo. Unsurprisingly, Ethiopian history has largely credited her spouse, Menelik II, for the historic defeat of the colonial Italians and erased her contribution. Thankfully, through the oral tradition and other first-hand accounts, I can share her story and we can all continue to learn from her vision and courage.

I was so inspired by her efforts I named my organization, Decolonize Design, after Empress Taytu's principled strategy, vision, and victory. We are guided by the philosophy of leveraging unique knowledges and strategy in both what we do and how we do it—prioritizing the struggle for dignity.

BELONGING, DIGNITY, JUSTICE, AND JOY

I can't remember when I was first introduced to diversity, equity, and inclusion (DEI) as a framework, but I vividly remember my initial response being "this is some bullshit." DEI is primarily an American framework for incorporating people who are not white heterosexual men into workplaces. As organizers, we focused our frameworks and learning on self-interest, values, and power. It wasn't until I left community organizing that I learned that the DEI framework was a prevailing way to engage Black and brown peoples in the workplace. I began to notice how DEI as a framework and practice was evangelized by many white professionals, specifically white women, who believed in DEI's potential to create equality for all people in the workplace.

How could a framework that defaults to and centers white dominant culture actually make the labor and life of non-whites better? Implicit in the DEI approach is accepting that whiteness is the standard we should be striving for and seeking inclusion into. What is wrong with this way of thinking? What dangerous tropes does it reinforce? What assumptions are made? Who created this framework? Why was it initially created? Why does the creator and messenger matter? Does whiteness or dominant culture represent achievement or success? Should it?

Though well-intentioned, DEI has not delivered and continues to not provide adequate return on investment. This is not by happenstance, but rather by design. The DEI industrial complex came into existence as a pre-emptive defense for avoiding litigation by members of protected classes, particularly under Title VII of the Civil Rights Act of 1964. For decades, the vast majority of Fortune 500 companies have implemented DEI train-ings, or other initiatives for their employees. The fact remains that these efforts have had minimal impact on reducing bias and have not yielded much in the way of qualitative behavior change or other desired changes in the workplace. Most disturbingly, DEI demands that we all internalize assimilation and compartmentalization of our true selves. We must see our lives as separate from our work, despite the fact that our social and political systems run our workplaces. Our intelligence is insulted when prevailing DEI approaches offer task-driven, representation-oriented views of organi-zation transformation. Those of us who are blessed with multiple identities know that every institution and system is connected and interdependent, especially the political and personal.

Tactics like trainings and audits often create more harm and trauma for the very group they are aimed to protect. For instance, a very popu-lar DEI approach focuses on "implicit bias trainings" that aim to expose the subconsciously held attitudes of anti-Blackness and racism in a work-place, but it offers little to overcome or mitigate the practical effects of these attitudes on those suffering from them in the workplace. Institutions have begun to rely on short-term training to bring long-lasting effects. These trainings may provide a convenient opportunity for employees participating in them to not take personal responsibility for their actions and instead look at the problem as a systemic issue beyond their control. The difficult work of changing beliefs and behaviors cannot be achieved with a series of trainings or by hiring more "diverse" candidates.

In addition to Empress Taytu, we also recall Sylvia Wynter, who encourages Black women to refuse to participate in a system of knowledge that has left us out. She called it *epistemic disobedience*. Wynter invites us to delink ourselves from systems and structures that leave out certain groups. Inherently a concept and framework like DEI classifies people by difference, requiring them to assimilate or remain outside of the system. Walter Mignolo suggests that Wynter's praxis is the decolonial option because it is:

> A practice of rethinking and unraveling dominant worldviews that have been opened up by Indigenous and black and Caribbean thinkers since the sixteenth century in América (with accent) and the Caribbean. The decolonial option does not simply protest the contents of imperial coloniality; it demands a delinking of oneself from the knowledge systems we take for granted (and can profit from) and practicing epistemic disobedience.

At Decolonize Design, we firmly reject that underlying premise of DEI and its mechanisms of coerced assimilation. We refuse settler colonial labels like "diverse" candidate and fight ideas like "representation" without justice. We are uninterested in investing in ways of thinking and being that doesn't uphold the dignity of us all. Reforming or adding to the current DEI framework was just not an option. Much like the "history" we are taught in public schools, the DEI framework was designed to default to the white settler colonial standard and logic, formally and informally. Our mission is to envision and create a more just and joyful world by interrogating the status quo and offering alternatives. To deliver on this mission, one alternative we offer is our Belonging, Dignity, Justice, and Joy (BDJJ) framework (pictured on the next page) to disrupt the superficial and harmful DEI initiatives that maintain the status quo. BDJJ speaks to our unique and sacred personhood while maintaining its roots in our collective humanity.

I start with the concept of belonging because to me, it is the feeling of being welcome as you are. Dignity, of course, is knowing that regardless of your status or station in life, you have inherent value that can never be denied. Justice is the vehicle and mechanism for repair; it's how we feel safe in uncertain situations knowing we can address harm and mistakes. Finally, joy, as we discussed earlier, is knowing you can celebrate and be celebrated wherever you are.

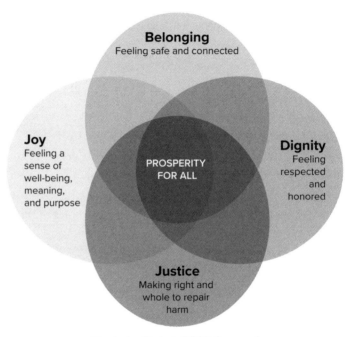

Decolonize Design's BDJJ framework

For many Black and Indigenous people, our critique and alternative framework offers language for dealing with a long-standing issue of assimilation and erasure, both rooted in a universal human experience while originating by centering African and Indigenous peoples. Built with guidance from the ancestors and elders as well as inspiration from Indigenous ways of knowing, BDJJ is a living framework with many meanings.

The sacred hoop, the four directions, or the medicine wheel is an Indigenous framework for health and healing. For different groups it has different meanings. For some the framework represents the stages in life, the seasons of the year, or the elements of nature. Even with many meanings and purposes the movement around this wheel follows the rise of the sun. This context is important as BDJJ is heavily inspired by this Indigenous tradition. Each piece of the framework is unique and important to the whole, all are mutually reinforcing—this Venn diagram symbolizes much more than the words on the page.

Almost daily, I receive messages from people from all walks of life asking to learn more about how to implement this framework in a workplace or community. They want to know if I can provide checklists or speak on how every organization can espouse BDJJ. But that's the problem, not everyone or every organization has the real appetite for transformation or the moral courage to move beyond (performative) actions to (embedded) behaviors. For that reason, I believe I have a duty to fight and a responsibility to protect the sacred and share our methods only with those who demonstrate a real commitment, care, and courage for people.

This is one of the most frequent questions I receive: How did you create it? It's important to note that this framework was not created in a day, or in a design sprint, or even in a linear fashion. This framework is a result of tension and resistance. Countless one-to-ones with strangers, long conversations with loved ones who pushed me to question everything, conferring with elder and ancestors (in spirit), and lots of solitude were a part of the recipe for this framework. And just like for a chef, knowing the list of ingredients and following a preparation guide isn't enough to create a special meal.

The second most popular question we receive is this: Does it work? And that expands to this: Do workplaces and communities really change once they have been exposed to BDJJ? That question requires that I pose a stage zero question: What do you mean by *work*? Does BDJJ solve the centuries of systemic, structural, and spiritual design elements of our settler colonial society? Hell no. Does it transform well-intentioned people of dominant groups so they become leaders of decolonization? Rarely. Is there a replicable, scalable way to bring this to every community? Enthusiastically, no.

The better question might be this: What does BDJJ in action look, feel, taste, sound, and smell like? Paint a literal and figurative picture to share a metaphor for the framework in action. Show me a neighborhood that is on the journey of BDJJ. These are all appropriate responses to better understand the mechanics and spiritual elements of this (and many other Indigenous frameworks) in practice. To learn more about this framework, we must be clear we've reached a shared understanding. The relational nature of this approach does not lend itself to becoming scaled or "viral." I believe I have a duty and responsibility to protect this sacred way of thinking and living.

We've discussed the DEI industrial complex, but that is just the beginning of our journey to expose, explore, and evolve our thinking on the status quo industries. Let's return to the design thinking industry introduced in "Part I: Re-member." The business and industry of design thinking is predicated on deficits that are politely reframed as "challenges." These challenges are typically responded to by the phrase "how might we," which is an approach that invites people to consider a solution together. This well-intentioned way to design spaces, places, people, and things offers short-term solutions at best and actively harmful solutions at its worst.

DESIGNING FOR BELONGING

As long as we are not ourselves, we will try to be what other people are.
—MALIDOMA PATRICE SOMÉ, writer and Dagara leader

It ends with love, exchange, fellowship. It ends as it begins, in motion, in between various modes of being and belonging, and on the way to new economies of giving, taking, being with and for and it ends with a ride in a Buick Skylark on the way to another place altogether.
—JACK HALBERSTAM, academic and writer

Belonging is a tricky word. In English, it has many meanings—two of which are seemingly contradictory. Belonging, of course, can mean feeling affinity, safety, membership, and care, but it can also mean being property and taking ownership. I offer to you that for our purposes, belonging means safety, care, and connection. Ensuring we have shared meaning and understanding is a critical step toward transformation and creation. Although most everything is designed, it is dangerous to rely on the same individuals or institutions who created the problem to provide solutions. Many of those responsible for the structural, systemic, and spiritual problems demonstrate a kind of historical amnesia and superficiality that often make problems worse.

Designing for Belonging, a project of the Stanford d.school, is especially ironic because the entire Stanford brand is based on exclusion and exploitation—from Leland Stanford, the founder of the university, who was openly racist and hostile to Black and Indigenous peoples, to many recent incidents of racial violence. This project is not only disingenuous, it's insulting, like putting lipstick on a pig to stay relevant and make money rather than grappling with the past in a meaningful way that addresses the university's role in exclusion and considering repair. Most importantly, it is spiritually and intellectually lazy for Stanford to reform its design thinking methodology without offering care, intention, and rigor to those most harmed by subjugation, exploitation, and violence. Designing for belonging, trauma-informed design, or any other buzzword of the moment (decolonization included!) is dangerous and reductive to a movement for real freedom. Trust me, I know from experience.

My organization, Decolonize Design, though well-intentioned and deliberate, is in some ways included in this critique. In 2018, when we were founded, our name and approach were routinely and pejoratively called "radical," "out of touch," and "extremist," but less than two years later, our moniker of Decolonize was a "metaphor" for anyone doing work in the social sector. We recognize the gravity and magnitude of the labor of decolonization. A core differentiator of our work and DEI practitioners generally is that our team of largely Black women inherited a world that erases, extracts, and exploits us—which means we lead by lived experience. We are working in and with communities to repair and reimagine a world worthy of our children. Our work began with a focus on community design, employing relational approaches. Beyond working with clients, we work to embody the inventive and distinct ways of working and being. In the time I've taken to write this book I have had an important revelation—one that changed the title of the book from *Decolonize Design to Kindred Creation* and that has spurred discussions on the name of the organization. Do we want to decolonize design? Is that our mission, to carry the work of reversing colonization? Is colonization our center? These questions are aimed at answering the critical question of what work or pursuit makes us feel alive and well.

Belonging begins with you. It is the act of putting your mask on first. If you have ever traveled by airplane, you likely know the safety instructions of "Put your mask on first before you assist others." Another related analogy is that you "can't pour from an empty cup." To experience belonging, we must know ourselves first. Too often, we are distracted with the harsh conditions we occupy and focus on basic survival. My life's work and the objective of this book is for Black people to resist showing up for everyone else and first see and know themselves.

Belonging is also a relationship. We belong to ourselves, our loved ones, the Earth, and the spirit world. Belonging is how we make relatives and kin. Belonging blossoms when the environment and conditions are fertile. You can belong to the land, a group of people, or a way of life. Belonging does not, however, mean making a home by erasure, theft, or forgetting. Take for instance, J. D. Vance's memoir *Hillbilly Elegy* where he describes Scots-Irish settlers finding belonging in the Appalachian Mountains that reminded them of home. Vance, who is now a venture capitalist and Republican senator who won his seat with the support of Trump, is fighting for settlers to belong. On the surface, this feeling of belonging sounds benign and functions to connect settlers to their homeland. The reality, however, of this kind of belonging is predicated on the removal and erasure of Black and Indigenous people, who were violently moved off of these mountains, and whose exploited labor made these states possible. Identifying as poor white (or as he calls his people *hillbillies*) doesn't preclude you from participating in the erasure of others, and in some ways it becomes a way out of taking responsibility for your ongoing role in colonization.

If we extend the metaphor of belonging to the feeling of being home, as offered in BDJJ, then the design of that home should begin with a reflection of what gives us comfort, care, safety, and joy. For me, feeling at home is not just four walls; it is also the smell of *itan* (frankincense), the sound of children giggling, access to a garden to pick fruit and veggies, and the sun's warmth on my skin. Home is a village. A neighborhood that is full of opportunity, resources, and caring people where everyone is valued and seen for their unique gifts. Some of these design elements are unique to me, whereas other elements might be widely accepted. Regardless of this vision's universal nature, what is most important is exploring your unique situation and context. To be very explicit, designing for belonging is not a scalable or plug-and-play activity; it is quite the opposite. It requires us to reckon and remember what *home* means, particularly when it was stolen, pillaged, or destroyed. We must consider all the ways home is described and defined by the oppressed, which very often is understood as a feeling, not a built environment.

Manhattan Beach, California, is a popular beach city in Los Angeles County. With the average beachfront property selling for more than $10 million, it is one of the most expensive places to live in the area. Not coincidentally, it has a population of less than 1 percent Black people. But it wasn't always that way. In 1920, a prime stretch of beachfront property in Manhattan Beach was the location of a Black resort called Bruce's Beach. This resort provided more than changing rooms and a restaurant. It was a refuge for Black people when they were not allowed on any other beach. While the built environment was beautiful and had function, what was most important about Bruce's Beach was how people felt. Black people felt safe, protected, and joyful. They could enjoy each other and the beauty of the beach without fear of harassment or harm. Charles and Willa Bruce created the resort precisely for that purpose—to provide safety and refuge for Black people as they enjoyed the beach. The refuge of Bruce's Beach did not last long because white neighbors, many of whom were Klansmen, began to harass the Black people who enjoyed the resort. Then, four years later, the city stole the land using eminent domain, claiming they wanted to use the land for a park.

Bruce's Beach is now a park with grassy knolls and a fire-fighting training facility. In 2020 California governor Gavin Newsom signed legislation to begin the return of Bruce's Beach to the Bruces' descendants with a very explicit intention of repairing and recognizing past harm. The property is not being given to the Bruce family, just returned. In 2022 it had a value of over $22 million. This return in property has material and symbolic value. While more than money was lost, some semblance of dignity was regained, and not just for Black people. In this case, the dignity of white people is also on the path of restoration as they reckon with the past and repair harm that has endured for hundreds of years. This is an example of how design can restore everyone's dignity, even the settlers.

The goal should be to create a place that recognizes, allows, and facilitates growth. There is no perfect place of belonging, nor can you make someone else feel like they belong. But by resisting oppressive and exploitative ways of being and working, we can spend time critically thinking about the world we live in and ways to employ kinship practices. In doing so, we design much more than individual belonging; we begin to design social movements, societies, and new world(s).

MY OFFERING: FROM REFUSAL TO RECIPROCITY AND FROM PRAXIS TO PROPHECY

What if beyond resistance is actually inaction? A place and space where we sit in silence, explore, and discover the invisible. Where isolation can breed innovation. Where sovereignty is a precursor to solidarity. Where we can integrate critical, conscious, and creative thinking and doing.

I hope by now we understand that there is no how-to, no recipe, no one-size-fits-all or program guaranteed to produce new ways of working and being. Instead, I submit that the journey to kinship and African knowledge is pursued with the intention of resistance. Resistance to the status quo, violence, exploitation, and all other forms of subjugation and harm. Every day and in every way, we must embody resistance as an experience and a practice. It is in these insurgent spaces that we can hope, dream, and escape without forgetting. Where we can escape danger and explore alternative worlds.

Resistance teaches us that the new world(s) require us to step away from cruelty and move to care. We must get curious about our past and our patterns individually and collectively. Explore our participation, or lack thereof, in a world of mutuality and reciprocity between humans, animals, and plants as necessary for true liberation from oppression.

Join me as we continue our journey to reclaim our individual and collective sacred personhood.

KEY READINGS

"Allen Iverson." *Players' Tribune*. Accessed December 18, 2023. https://www
.theplayerstribune.com/articles/life-and-times-of-allen-iverson.

Benjamin, Ruha. *Viral Justice: How We Grow the World We Want*. Princeton, NJ:
Princeton University Press, 2024.

Christianopoulos, Dinos. *The Body and the Wormwood* (1960–1993), trans. Nicholas
Kostis, 1995.

Glissant, Edouard. *The Poetics of Relation*. Trans. Betsy Wing. Ann Arbor, MI:
University of Michigan Press, 1997.

Guilfoyle, Ultan, dir. *Frank Gehry: Building Justice*. United States, 2018, film.

Hersey, Tricia. *Rest Is Resistance: A Manifesto*. New York: Little, Brown Spark, 2022.

hooks, bell and George Yancy. "bell hooks: Buddhism, the Beats and Loving
Blackness." *New York Times*, December 10, 2015. https://archive.nytimes.com
/opinionator.blogs.nytimes.com/2015/12/10/bell-hooks-buddhism-the-beats
-and-loving-blackness/.

Jemisin, N. K. *The City We Became*. London: Orbit, 2021.

Kelley, Robin D. G. *Freedom Dreams: The Black Radical Imagination*. Boston, MA:
Beacon Press, 2022.

Lorde, Audre. "The Uses of Anger." Keynote speech at the National Women's
Studies Association Conference, Storrs, Connecticut, June 1981.

Mignolo, Walter D. "Sylvia Winter: What Does It Mean to Be Human?" in *Sylvia
Winter: On Being Human as Praxis*, ed. Katherine McKittrick, Durham, NC:
Duke University Press, 2015.

The Nap Ministry. https://thenapministry.wordpress.com/about/

Ogden, Stormy. "What Was My Crime? Being an American Indian Woman,"
in *Neo-Colonial Injustice and the Mass Imprisonment of Indigenous Women*, eds. Lily
George, Adele N. Norris, Antje Deckert, Juan Tauri, 173–191. Palgrave
Studies in Race, Ethnicity, Indigeneity, and Criminal Justice. Basingstoke, UK:
Palgrave Macmillan, 2020.

Pater, Ruben. *Caps Lock: How Capitalism Took Hold of Graphic Design, and How to Escape from It*. Amsterdam, Netherlands: Valiz, 2021.

Perry, Imani. *Prophets of the Hood: Politics and Poetics in Hip Hop*. Durham, NC: Duke University Press, 2004.

Rhoden, William C. *Forty Million Dollar Slaves: The Rise, Fall, and Redemption of the Black Athlete*. New York: Three Rivers Press, 2010.

Rogers, Mary Beth. *Cold Anger: A Story of Faith and Power Politics*. College Station, TX: Texas A & M University Press, 2006.

Sayers, Daniel O. *A Desolate Place for a Defiant People: The Archaeology of Maroons, Indigenous Americans, and Enslaved Laborers in the Great Dismal Swamp*. Gainesville, FL: University Press of Florida, 2015.

Wilson, Shawn. *Research Is Ceremony: Indigenous Research Methods*. Black Point, Nova Scotia: Fernwood Publishing, 2021.

Birth as the Portal

Aida Mariam Davis

I live in a painfully paradoxical world where I am
weak yet threatening,
disabled yet immune to pain,
ultimately unworthy of care and concern
Counterfeits lay claim to "care" but it's really just careless
Naively I demand more visibility and still
visibility don't give me vision

Visibility merely puts me on display
to the white gaze
unreal but powerful
that colonizes my community
Give me radical vision to see what is invisible to others

Birthing is a ticket and invitation
to transport us all
in a body, never alone
Bloody and Breathless is our first home
The womb is our pro-vision

Before I became a mother
I was a revolutionary
before I was a revolutionary
I was a **black sheep**, a pariah and an outsider
Expelled, pushed out—it's the only way through

Birthing is a way of structuring our world
it is the courage
to conceive and care for new life
and claim new light
to be pregnant with freedom

To love on our kin and neighbors
a parable of beloved community
An anthem of new possibilities for more intimate connections
The powerful allegory of how we see ourselves,
our potential,
and our legacy

In this new life, we welcome the Spirit home.

PART III

RECLAIM

RETURN TO
RIGHT RELATIONSHIP

Ubuntu

Translation: I am because we are

The worldview of *ubuntu* is an African philosophy of relational personhood. According to the Zulu, people are not people without relationships with other people. In other words, a newborn baby is not a person on their own but is a person because of their interaction with their parents, siblings, animals, neighbors, the spirit, and the dearly departed. It is once they establish these relationships that they realize their selfhood. African knowledge is fundamentally a dialog. Our understanding changes depending on our relationship with the person sharing the knowledge. Using this logic, so much of what is understood by you, the reader, is largely based on the degree to which you connect with me.

Ancestor and writer Audre Lorde reclaims the ubuntu wisdom in the Black American context in "Poetry Is Not a Luxury" when she says, "The white fathers told us: I think, therefore I am. The Black mother within each of us—the poet—whispers in our dreams: I feel, therefore I can be free . . . Our children cannot dream unless they live, they cannot live unless they are nourished." She goes on to explain that it is these same white fathers that want us to continually look for problems to be solved and rely only on our ideas to make us free. But if we reflect on our ancestral Black and African way of life, we understand that the art and science of living is an experience of cherishing ourselves and respecting the hidden sources of power within ourselves and our communities. We abandon the obsession with so-called facts and data and begin to value feelings and spiritual revelation. We treasure poetry as the distillation of feelings and the lifeline for our existence. Lorde goes on to describe poetry as imagination plus insight, the power to name the nameless and transform ideas into action. To me, poetry is a location for collective memory and consciousness while it responds to alienation and domination. This is why poetry is not a luxury, it is dangerous and formidable—making it one of the greatest threats to settler colonialism and capitalism.

In the tradition of my elders and ancestors, Lorde uses poetry and prose to give deep meaning to the dark places that hold our strength and power.

Darkness, it turns out, is required for all things to rest and grow. One of the first dark places we, as humans, experience is the womb. Birthing people understand first-hand the places of power and possibility that interconnect people. While conceiving and growing another human, we become, as Lorde writes,

> Sanctuaries and fortresses and spawning grounds for the most radical and daring of ideas, the house of difference so necessary to change and the conceptualization of any meaningful action. Right now, I could name at least ten ideas I would have once found intolerable or incomprehensible and frightening, except as they came after dreams and poems. This is not idle fantasy, but the true meaning of "it feels right to me." We can train ourselves to respect our feelings, and to discipline (transpose) them into a language that matches those feelings so they can be shared. And where that language does not yet exist, it is our poetry which helps to fashion it. Poetry is not only dream or vision, it is the skeleton architecture of our lives.

Interconnectedness and interdependence, it seems, begin with introspection and relating to our own feelings. As a Black woman I understand the power of feelings and the reality that feelings are not meant to survive—not in a settler colonial context, not in a patriarchal context, and certainly not in a capitalistic context. Poems stir emotion and insight, and as a result, motivate action. It is through poems we can gather strength and courage to be daring and ultimately access our power. Poetry is an African feminist necessity to reclaiming ourselves and each other.

It is important you and I share an understanding on the meaning of the word *reclaim* before we explore the weight and work of reclaiming ourselves and the world. On one hand, reclaim means to recover or return something that was stolen or lost. On the other hand, reclaim means to bring under cultivation. Lorde poetically utilizes both definitions to nurture the future. We, too, will be using both definitions as we continue on our journey.

If you've read this book in a linear fashion, you know that we've discussed the many ways to recall, resist, and otherwise respond to the inherited settler-native-enslaved relationship as a past and present experience. In this section, we explore ways to create and reclaim what was our first nature. One of the core differences between Black and settler colonial approaches to design and creation is that Indigenous traditions acknowledge the presence of the spirit and integrate it into our knowledge systems.

Together, you and I can acknowledge the spirit here. In doing so, we can be originators and create new things that break the binary and embrace the spirit. Too often, design (in its many definitions) has meant relating to or reflecting settler dominant values. Kindred creation is not about redefining or reshaping that kind of design, it is about reclaiming who we are (and who we've always been) without the imposition of settler society, and it is about stewarding African Indigenous cultural practices and wisdoms.

Kindred creation goes radically to the root to understand circumstances, to create new kin, to study and struggle together, and most importantly, to care for each other's spiritual development.

As we continue to travel together, I hope you feel our deepening connection. I've shared my personal stories, insights, and learnings with you for your thoughtful consideration. Now, I'd like to take you a little bit closer into one of the most significant, sacred, beautiful moments of my life—my marriage ceremony. Marriage is a ritual and rite of passage that represents a transformation of individuals, families, and societies. It is an initiation in which two people form a union and that union transforms a village, which is why, in Ethiopian tradition, marriage is not only an individual choice but a kinship one.

Let me be clear, though, marriage is not a perfect institution, and over time, with the mingling of capitalism and colonialism, it has become an oppressive one. One that has the potential to erase and monetize people. So many of our sacred events are marred in this way. And this was the main reason why, at a very young age, I never wanted to marry. I hated playing house and I really hated the teenage daydreaming about walking down the aisle. I noticed how many women like me lost their power and sense of self once married, and I just couldn't afford any more oppression.

I did, however, dream of a life partner. Someone I admired, respected, learned from, loved unconditionally, and could raise children with. Through magic, manifestation, and a miracle—I met my husband. He, like many of the Black feminists in my life, has held me accountable to my values, nurtured my mind and spirit, and pushed me to my potential. He shows me through example what integrity, playfulness, and mental toughness look, feel, taste, sound, and smell like every day. In our relationship, I am able to reclaim parts of myself that I banished after the pain of failed relationships. With him, I began to revisit my deep connection to African Indigenous philosophies and the multitudinous forms of the blessing of Blackness.

At AfroPunk Paris, a festival that celebrates and showcases the radical thought and social nonconformity of the African diaspora globally, Reggie and I found a special place of freedom. On that trip, we continued on to Morocco, Zanzibar, and Ethiopia. All places where we spiritually felt the psychological safety and freedom in our Blackness. That feeling and friendship (and fun) were and are the emotions that I wanted to replicate in all aspects of my life, including my wedding. After that trip, it was not long until I birthed Decolonize Design and Reggie proposed to me.

Our wedding, from the outset, was designed to be hella Black. My husband and I were both inspired by Nikki Giovanni's words "Black love is Black wealth," and this became our guiding planning principle. We chose the Historic 16th Street Station in Oakland, the location of the West Coast headquarters of the Brotherhood of Sleeping Car Porters—the first Black union in the country. We invited our ancestors, both figuratively and literally; we designated a table for ancestors with photos and descriptions. I wore a gown by an Ethiopian designer, the late Amsale Aberra, and traditional Ethiopian jewelry. Our officiant was a family elder, Fania Davis, who presided in majestic and multicultural form. She conjured the wisdom of ubuntu to emphasize the purpose of our marriage as she shared,

It is not just two individuals who give all of themselves to one another. We are who we are because of our relationships—with families, communities, and the larger collective of humanity and the earth. This is the meaning of the southern African proverb of Ubuntu.

And so with Aida's and Reggie's beautiful union as individuals, entire families and ancestral lineages also join together. And, we, the families and communities of the bride and groom, also give ourselves to one another.

We rejoice and celebrate today both the giving of all of themselves to one another and also the giving of all ourselves to another.

She continued,

Aida, your beautiful Ethiopian family is joining Reggie's beautiful Black American family. The coming together of these families begins to heal the wounds inflicted by the Middle Passage on both sides of the Atlantic. It is not lost upon us that in 2019, the 400th anniversary of the beginning of slavery in this country, we are re-establishing the bonds that were broken by honoring the union of these two persons today. This wedding is thus both an act of healing and an act of liberation.

So, it turns out I don't hate weddings or marriage. In fact, I love the symbolism, intention, and ritual—I just hate oppression and commodification. Weddings are rituals of renewal. At our wedding, all members of the community were involved, including parents, children, siblings, servers, and custodians. All in attendance witnessed the collective investment in our future. At the very end of the ceremony, in our gown and tuxedo, we knelt to ask the elders for their blessing and advice.

Our wedding marked the beginning of an intentional relationship that has a foundation in safety, care, and culture. My union and growing family intensified my pursuit of creating a world worthy of our children. Every day together, as a family, is an invitation for us to establish a deeper sense of self-regard and elicit revelation and to offer access to divinity in order to transform. Reclaiming our relationships, intimate and platonic, first requires us to understand our interconnectedness and interdependence on this planet.

I submit to you that the ultimate goal of kindred creation is to be in *right relations*—that is, to step into the duties of being in relationship with others (human, nonhuman, and nature). This desperate need for right relations is evidenced by our global climate crisis. What we are experiencing is more than a catastrophe of our ecosystems and biodiversity, it is a problem with our fundamental relationship with the Earth. The impact of being out of right relations is a third-wave kind of colonization in which oppressed peoples are geographically displaced, food systems are destroyed, and cultures are becoming eradicated. With a full-picture view of the role and ongoing impact of settler colonialism, we understand that climate change is not an isolated environmental issue that can be remedied by reducing greenhouse gas emissions but a crisis of relationship. The kind that requires discontinuing incremental colonial relations. We must move ourselves into integration with global ecosystems and kinship with all lifeforms.

Thankfully, I am not alone in this pursuit of creating and improving our world of relations. Editors Gavin Van Horn, Robin Wall Kimmerer, and John Hausdoerffer extensively explore the living world's deep interconnection in the five-part series *Kinship: Belonging in a World of Relations*. The *Kinship* volumes—*Planet, Place, Partners, Persons, Practice*—offer essays, interviews, poetry, and stories of solidarity, highlighting the interdependence and interconnectedness of our world. Through cosmologies, narratives, and everyday interactions, readers are invited to embrace a world that acknowledges the Indigenous responsiveness and responsibility. The African context extends understanding of kin not only as a noun but as a verb—the activity of creating new, caring relationships.

This section of reclaim is where we connect history, heritage, and home—three critical elements of kinship. To begin this section, let us revisit "The Parable of the Tree." Trees, like people, evolve, learn, and adapt their behaviors with intention and deep connection. This sororal kinship of trees is rooted in the Mother Tree, the old-growth matriarch that acts as a hub of nutrients for trees of different ages and species. The Mother Tree is mysterious, majestic, and magical in how she connects and sustains the complex tree society. She is the center of communication, protection, and sentience for her kin. This care and concern continue even after she dies. In her transition, she leaves an inheritance of wisdom and knowledge about how to live in an ever-evolving world. This is no different than my mothering or the mothering of parents, other mothers, and village mamas.

All of us, and especially those who are caregivers, must explore our own mystery, magic, and majesty. These are the gifts we receive at birth. I believe my gifts are a unique vision and provision to share ideas. These gifts engendered confidence and commitment, enabling me to resist assimilation and conformity.

Spiritually, I know I can transform the world through my often-underestimated existence. I encourage you to take time right now, as you read this, to consider what your unique gifts are. Think about what makes you come alive or what makes you feel fully yourself.

It's important to note that our gifts are not always parts of ourselves we've embraced or parts others have celebrated.

This journey to reclaim ourselves, our relatives, and our world requires deliberate and intentional moral courage. Settler colonialism and capitalism can't survive when you discover yourself and live with intention. The central obstacle to reclaiming our Indigenous knowledges and way of life is distraction. Whether it is spending most of our waking hours working, or scrolling mindlessly on social media, exploitation and programming can thrive when we don't know ourselves. Embracing our complex selves moves us from transaction to transformation.

In my own search for self-determination and freedom, I've experienced many revelations. I've realized kindred creation is more than form and function; it is fundamentally about how people, places, and practices feel. Kindred creation, much like community organizing, is both an art and a science. Kindred creation, much like creating new life, is conceiving, birthing, and caring for each other as precious gifts. Reclaiming creation, then, begins with engaging our complete selves, emotionally, spiritually, politically, physically, psychologically, and intellectually.

Reclaiming creation, like the cycle of life, ends and begins with revelation—a supernatural understanding to continue the journey. When we explore the spirit and supernatural, we learn that questions are more important than answers. That which we are questioning asks us to experience an adventure to someplace new, where we can experience fullness, multiplicity, and new ways of being.

PREGNANT WITH POSSIBILITY: CONCEIVING AND BEARING

It is our divine human nature to create life and give life, whether through mind, body, or soul.

Nurturing Relationships and Resistance

All of us were conceived, carried, and birthed. This journey that begins in the womb is the first experience where we are intimately connected and reliant on someone else for all our needs. This birthing person has had the courage to conceive and commit to bringing new life, no matter the circumstances. Not all of us can birth children, but we can all birth new life. The precious and precarious time of pregnancy is unlike any other time in the human experience.

For me, this was especially true on January 7, 2020—the day it was confirmed I was growing new life in my womb. Long before I became pregnant, I knew that the responsibility and blessing of caring for a child would be my highest calling. Since I was a child, I had looked forward to the day when I could be a parent, in part because I wanted to correct the harm I had experienced and to create a home and lifestyle that affirms and cherishes who my children are.

Both parent and child are transformed by the experience of pregnancy. In the unique physiological processes that take place during pregnancy, the boundaries between human beings are blurred. The production of a new person through a deeply intimate process can not only radically transform the pregnant person's body, but also their understanding, values, and who and what they take themselves to be. It is the heavy responsibility of the pregnant person not only to care for themselves but for the fetus. Their existence and bodies are inextricably linked. In many other settings, this interdependence is called solidarity. Frequently, pregnancy, birth, and mothering are characterized as feminine experiences and therefore dismissed, undermined, and unappreciated for the radical and transformative work that goes into creating new life.

Gestation is the nucleus of a series of intricate and inimitable processes within reproduction: conception, pregnancy itself, birth, post-natal recovery, and breastfeeding. These key aspects of human life are underinvestigated and researched in how pregnancy plays a role in our daily lives. Disciplines like design, that are not coincidentally dominated by men, often do not investigate these processes. That is because such processes do not fit neatly into the paradigm of science or design as discrete independent disciplines with firm boundaries. Pregnancy, birth, and early motherhood inescapably involve issues of gender, race, and class. Most people who undergo these physiological processes identify as women. Gender expectations contribute to how we understand the duties of pregnant people and mothers. However, not all persons who are pregnant, give birth, or lactate identify as women or as mothers, and not all mothers experience pregnancy, birth, or lactation. As we work to create a world of kindred relations, we must rethink these key conceptual schemes.

For all of my first pregnancy, the United States was still under the harsh regime of the Trump administration and experiencing the global syndemic of Covid-19, anti-Blackness, and settler colonialism. Under these conditions, I was terrified of bringing a Black child into this world. I knew a bit about navigating the world as a Black child in a hostile, occupied environment, but no one could have prepared me for what unfolded during 2020. From shelter-in-place, to televised, state-sanctioned murders of Black people, to exacerbated income inequity, to isolated labor and delivery—I was in a perpetual state of shock, anxiety, and trauma. At a personal level, I was fighting. Fighting to be heard by my OBGYN and healthcare providers, fighting to advocate for a radical new way of working with Decolonize Design, fighting to maintain privacy and at the same time seeking care from extended family.

For so many birthing people, particularly Black birthing people, the omnipresence of denial, dismissal, and gaslighting is familiar. Thankfully, the words of my elders (and prophetic writers) Alice Walker and Assata Shakur remind me that the plotting and fighting are a necessary part of my self-actualization. The push and pull of these many challenges demanded I stay with my humanity and bloom in rebellion against the harsh circumstances. In his poem *The Rose That Grew from Concrete*, poet and philosopher Tupac Shakur reminds us that the rose can not only grow in the concrete, but it can also walk and dream. Shakur offers us a metaphor of what it's like to be an oppressed person in America. He begins by asking the reader about a very unlikely situation of a rose growing in a hostile environment, one that is designed to suffocate its life, making the rose's very existence a miracle. He continues to disorient the reader by declaring that "it learned to walk without having feet." He goes on to draw attention to the irony that the rose has the audacity to dream and in doing so can find a lifeline to continue to grow.

Tupac Shakur's poetry reminds me that the world, as it is, is not as it should be. Repeatedly he assures us that, despite the collective gaslighting we as oppressed peoples might experience, or the distractions put in our way, we must stay true to ourselves, our mission, and our mutuality. Most importantly, we must continuously resist the notion that dominant culture can define us and coerce us into assimilation. The rose is a magical being that, in spite of its inherited place, can transform itself and the world around it. The rose remembers its purpose and stays true to its spirit of resistance because the magic we possess is not to be spent on conforming. And what we experience as marvelous and magic cannot be defined by settler norms and logic.

Since the start of settler society, settlers have placed an unhealthy emphasis on and had an obsession with technology. Settler way of life demands that we do more, and do it efficiently, so that we rely on products more than people. The tradeoff, however, is valuing products and profits over people. The myopic and often patriarchal focus leaves the designs of the natural world out of view. Take, for instance, settler societies' interest and investment in the field of artificial intelligence (AI). AI is predicated on idea that computers can perform tasks better than human intelligence. And yet, breast- and chestfeeding utilize a kind of intelligence that is outside the human mind. Breastfeeding is a critical phase of human development, for both parent and baby, in that it provides nourishment, protection, and deep emotional attachment. The magic of breastfeeding lies in the way the human body learns, responds, and creates for other humans. Breastmilk restructures itself for a unique set of antibodies, leukocytes, and nutrients to support the baby. Breastmilk even changes its taste and composition to promote infant sleep. Breastmilk sustains life and its creation offers lessons on the magic of the body, mothering (and gender-neutral ways of nurturing), and the gift of human connection. This contrast between how little is known about human breastfeeding with the proliferation of AI shows us the priorities and focus of settler ways.

Birthing and Rebirth

> *Every story I create, creates me. I write to create myself.*
> —OCTAVIA BUTLER, Afrofuturist and author

When I experienced birth and witnessed the miracle and gift of life, I was overcome with a joy and love that can only be described as supernatural. I was lifted from unrelenting pain and focused on nurturing this new being and protecting them from all danger. It occurred to me, though, that while this is a momentous experience for me, it is even more significant for the baby. The day they were born is the first day they experienced humans outside the muffled space of the womb, and over the course of a few days, the first time they experience the warmth of the sun, the sounds and sights of their new home, and the nourishment of breastmilk and formula. As a parent, guide, and caregiver, it is my responsibility to be their shepherd of wonder. To offer seemingly quotidian experiences, like pausing to sit in a grass field and talk to the grass as a friend, or presenting ideas that might challenge their implicit beliefs—all so that they may find meaning on their own terms.

Birth marks an important moment in African life. It is the moment when an individual begins to express their sense of identity and belonging. It is when a people become kin, community members, and future ancestors. Birth is an important portal. A vital necessity, a light with which to access our hopes and dreams for survival and change. A child is born; never alone or without connection—always rooted to the soil, ancestors, and community. Griots and ritual keepers, such as Sobonfu Somé, recall stories of all the ways children enter our communities. Even before conception, Africans feel the child's spirit and await their arrival so that they may welcome their spirit home. It is understood that the children are here to teach us necessary lessons from the universe. Through language and imagery, birth has also been used as a vehicle to offer insight into other concepts, usually new, complex, or controversial. Often, representations of birth are metaphors for creativity or beginnings. In many holy texts and creation stories, birth metaphors are central to the narrative. In more recent texts, Black writers and other artists have employed birth imagery to address issues like war, poverty, and patriarchy.

Octavia Butler, a writer who birthed a dozen science fiction books, understood the mutual transformation of creation. After being discouraged by her family members and told that Black girls can't be writers, and after publishers rejected many of her books, she kept creating. She took odd jobs, like working as a potato chip inspector, to support herself while she wrote her novels. And even after she published, receiving criticism from the *New York Times* that said her novels were "evocative" and "often troubling," she continued to create. It seems she had a prophetic vision that once written, offered her courage and commitment. While she often incorporated critiques of the future and technology, I don't think she could anticipate what Black people are experiencing now.

Artificial intelligence on the other hand, has its sights on creating technologies that respond and learn in a similar way to humans. It has captivated the imagination of corporations as they are investing an incredible amount of money in AI because to them, it represents the future. And yet, from my vantage point, it represents the future of settler societies. In the American context, bias, anti-Blackness, and ableism have already been exposed as critical, and in some cases deadly, limitations of AI. Are we creating or participating in an evolved and self-sustaining settler future? Are we accelerating the erasure of African and Indigenous ways of being, doing, and behaving in community?

Globally, AI has been promoted as necessary technology for the future of our communities and the products that we interface with daily. For many Indigenous people like me, AI represents a dystopian future with opportunities for even greater oppression and exploitation. Building machines that display intelligence rather than learning from our bodies represents our values and priorities. How can artificial intelligence mean more to humanity and the planet than the human body and spirit? It is bewildering to think that the way machines learn and respond to information is more important and impressive than the ways we create and sustain the natural world.

Reclaiming a future free of settler (technological) colonialism requires that we grapple with key questions:

- Who is creating this? Why are they creating it?

- What knowledge system are we employing? Why?

- What information do we value? Why?

- Why are we more impressed by artificial intelligence than the human body and spirit? Whose knowledge is deemed valid?

- How is this way of thinking gendered?

- What other possibilities exist outside of our current way of knowing and being?

Then, once we've asked and answered these questions, we can conceive, prepare, and plan for a world of kindred connections and creation. One where our creations are motivated by a desire to become relatives and kin. The practice of improving, inspiring, or acting on a divine message is a critical component to birthing new life and kin. Whatever the motivation to create, gestation and conception are powerful, sometimes painful experiences. For African people, particularly those living on occupied land, this experience is especially difficult. That is why the work to birth and usher in new life is a collective endeavor supported and attended to by doulas, midwives, practitioners, and partners. Together, we can birth and nurture the kin, community, and society that recognizes the labor and love birthing people offer.

In a world that has attempted to sterilize Black and Indigenous women, birthing is an act of survival for generations to come. Birthing is dangerous. Not just because of the possibility of death during the process, but because the alternative of not creating new life could mean an end of kin or community death—the extinction of traditions, cultures, and in some cases, nations. Feminist Cree scholar Kim Anderson elaborates in her contribution to *Indigenous Women and Feminism* (Suzack et al.), "Affirmations of an Indigenous Feminist": "As mothers of the nations, Indigenous women are supposed to be revered for birthing the upcoming generations and for being their first teachers. Women are also said to be carriers of the culture—a responsibility that we have by virtue of our connection to the very young." African and Indigenous women understand our sacred role. And yet, we also understand first-hand how precarious and invisible our creations might appear to settler society, but we continue to create. I have realized that freedom and healing depend on us working to usher in the gift of new life and our inherent responsibility to steward and nurture.

Most people associate kinship with biological relationships between families, clans, and tribes, but birth and kinship do not require blood relations or biological connections. Kinship only requires connection and commitment. Kinship for Africans across the diaspora is often preserved by women. The quintessential nurturing relationship is that of "mothering," and yet laced into the cultural understanding are oppressive gender norms, exploitation, and endless sacrifice. In Black communities, where mass incarceration, racism, and poverty often intersect, mothers must work double duty to provide for their family. In such situations, "other-mothers," or village mothers, step in to share caregiving responsibilities. Other-mothers are the network of people—relatives, neighbors, and friends—a biological mother can rely on. This model of kinship, informed by West African traditions, is a collective approach to intimacy and care. The Black Panther Party, the Combahee River Collective, and the AIDS Coalition to Unleash Power (ACT UP) organizations all created communities of care or families of choice as powerful forms of kinship by offering mutual aid and care for people settler society has oppressed.

I submit to you that your family—whether blood or chosen, human or nonhuman, past or current or future—is your kin and requires your care. Whether you are creating new people, projects, or practices, you and your relatives rely on your ongoing commitment to reclaiming lost or stolen parts of yourself. Birthing and rebirthing ourselves and our kin bring into focus two critical elements of returning to right relationship—time and place.

African Time: Time Is Vertical

The first time I visited Ethiopia was Meskerem 2000 (known in America as September 2007). Ethiopia does not follow the Gregorian calendar and instead employs another calculation of time. It is one of very few countries in the world to reject the settler way of accounting for time. Meskerem, the 13th month in the Ethiopian calendar, coincides with the end of the rains in Ethiopia; it is associated with harvest and renewal. It is also understood as liminal—a time when the spirit visitations happen and a time of year that is neither the old year and nor the new.

It was there, in Ethiopia, that I began to deeply understand that time is not universal or linear in movement. I planned this trip *back home* in complete defiance of and disobedience to my parents' wishes since they believed it was a dangerous time to visit alone. At that time, I was a recent college graduate. I felt it was important for me to experience my ancestral homeland and apply all that I learned in my Black Studies classes. Most importantly, I was aching to meet relatives, touch ground on my motherland, and celebrate the Ethiopian New Year (September 11th).

I arrived in late August and I spent every day leading up to September 11th at a new relative's home in a different part of town. Each neighborhood I visited, from Bole to Merkato to Kazanchis, while very different in many ways, shared the African cultural reality and tradition of a different time. I observed my relatives to be conscious of their environment and aware of the spirit and the nature around them as they told time and oriented themselves. It reminded me of Nigerian writer Chinua Achebe's *Things Fall Apart* in which he refers to the African concept of time as being related to the moon, the harvest, and the planting seasons. In the first pages of the book, Achebe describes the protagonist Okonkwo working daily on his farm from cock crow until the chickens went to roost. Again, a few pages later, he writes that Ikemefuna came to Umuofia at the end of the carefree season, between harvest and planting. This understanding of time, as contextual and tied to events, is not limited to West Africa but spans beyond the continent to Indigenous cultures around the globe.

John Mbiti, an African philosopher, claims time is of little concern to the thought system of Africans. To Mbiti, and most Africans, time is radically contextual. A series of nonlinear narratives, which have occurred, are also currently taking place, and in the immediate sense, will occur. What many categorize as the future, he suggests, falls in the category of "no time." African time, as Mbiti insinuates, is defined by Africans' love of the past and value of the present with little interest in the distant future. The rational and mechanical time as America and Europe standardizes it, does not define time for the Africans; rather, as Achebe writes, time is intimately linked with events, rituals, natural cycles, and the supernatural.

This perspective may seem to come into conflict with the Iroquois wisdom of planning for seven generations, Afrofuturism, or religious beliefs. These forward-looking practices, musings, and beliefs also exist in the African perspective that Mbiti describes. The way many Africans cultivate and harvest food employs ancestral wisdom that plans for and anticipates many generations to come. Magical realism and imagination are cultural hallmarks of all African folklore across the continent. Very importantly, African time inherently connects to the spiritual realm, as an experience we can simultaneously inhabit in the present and beyond is a cornerstone to many African faith traditions. Looking deeply at epistemologies can be a powerful way to make connections to how oppressed people understand time and opt out of settler binary thinking.

In the American context, Black and settler cultural conceptions of time differ in consequential ways. When we consider the origin and role of jazz music, we see how settler culture asserts that a linear development of a song leads to its closure. It is this predictable progression that defines music. By these standards, jazz is outside and does not fit. Settler and Eurocentric beliefs dictate that rhythmic repetition and improvisation are associated with savagism, primitivity, and nature. Poetically, it is improvisation and call-and-response patterns that connect jazz music to Africa. Jazz's improvisation and rhythmic timing represents an energy, freedom, and reclamation of Black diasporic music.

No matter how we orient to time, it shapes our everyday lives. Time, and its organization, are significant concepts for all humanity. It is a dimension that structures all that we know about our species, and contrary to the settler structure, time is not homogeneous, universal, or linear. As Native philosopher Viola F. Cordova observes in *How It Is*, "time is an abstraction derived from the fact that there is motion and change in the world." Like whiteness, the notion and the experience of time are socially constructed and, therefore, historically and culturally variable. Time is not under the dominance or control of human beings; it is not something to be shaped or filled.

In my assessment, time is a dimension of the surrounding world, including nature and the spirit world. It is a dimension that marks our collective and divergent process of becoming. Looking for patterns and predicting current conditions allows us to traverse a less-explored approach to design and creation—one that roots us in the present. That is not to say there is no future or that futurism has no place; in fact, I am suggesting that two things can be true despite appearing to conflict. I affirm that divergent approaches can, in fact, live together without submitting to binary/either-or settler thinking.

Scholar Mark Rifkin brings into focus the implications of settler time in his book *Beyond Settler Time: Temporal Sovereignty and Indigenous Self*. He explains the nuance of time, orientation, and our sense of self:

> Self-determination appears less as a particular and properly modern mode of performing peoplehood than as the expression of the multiplicity of Indigenous peoples' ways of being and becoming. To speak of Indigenous orientations suggests processes of being and becoming that emerge out of everyday life. They arise from, among other things, memory, storying, collective practices, dynamics of maturation and family formation, modes of inhabitation and connections to place, encounters with law and policy in their quotidian effects, histories of dispossession and opposition to it, and engagements with nonhuman entities of various kinds.

Reclaiming time and orientation is a sacred and fundamental element for self-determination and sovereignty. According to Sara Ahmed's *Queer Phenomenology*, to be oriented, to know where you are in space and time, is to find your own direction in life. Another way to think of orientation is to imagine a room that you've lived in for ten years. You are likely familiar with every item, fixture, and object in that space, and you can likely navigate the space with ease and confidence. This kind of orientation exists for African people who live in their ancestral homelands; they have intrinsic knowledge of the land, water, air, plants, and wildlife of that place. Ancestors, for instance, play an important part in the daily life of many African and Indigenous peoples. These spiritual and cultural rituals exist outside of settler frame of time because they do not originate or are not enforced by settler ways.

The Māori people, much like Ethiopians, offer another example of people reclaiming time and releasing the way of the colonizer. Guided by their belief of day-to-day practices of regeneration, revitalization, and decolonization in culture and society, they have decided to begin to opt out of settler time. The Gregorian calendar introduced by settlers, does not consider environment, ecology, location, culture, or cultural nuances in its account. By following a different calendar, one that is based on astronomy, the position of the sun, and the phases of the moon, the Māori can explore Indigenous knowledge systems as pathways to more sustainable forms of living. For settlers, time has been the vehicle for colonization, industrialization, globalization, and capitalism; by creating a singular "universal" time, settlers have created time geared toward marketplace and industry. The Māori understanding of time rejects the idea that time is universal and it must be monitored, monetized, or saved, as explained in the American maxim "time is money." Rather than counting time like coins, the Māori account of time is concerned with "living time."

Another dimension to time is one that originates from lived experience, like the concept of crip time. Ellen Samuels, professor and a founding member of the University of Wisconsin Disability Studies Initiative, explains in her essay *Six Ways of Looking at Crip:*

> For crip time is broken time. It requires us to break in our bodies and minds to new rhythms, new patterns of thinking and feeling and moving through the world. It insists that we listen to our body-minds so closely, so attentively, in a culture that tells us to divide the two and push the body away from us while also pushing it beyond its limits. Crip time means listening to the broken languages of our bodies, translating them, honoring their words.

What would time feel like if it prioritized and protected caregiving? What if we collectively understood crip time? Or prioritized creativity, children, or feelings like grief? Children make weird and wondrous use of time. Creativity thrives where there is freedom. And grief is best understood expressed rather than suppressed.

Is it possible to totally reclaim alternative ways of telling time? Absolutely. Time is an orientation to the world and to life. We can protect time rather than fill it. Time does not have to mean money; we can uncouple it from capitalistic and colonial norms. We can reflect seasonal or episodic time; either way, we can choose to orient it around a different axis with different priorities.

Operating in cooperation with the settler society reinforces and offers legitimacy to their occupation. In the Black community, we often joke about Colored People (CP) time, and perhaps, that is a reclaimed or alternative way of engaging with time that rejects that settler legitimacy. By slowing down and resting, we can collect parts of ourselves we neglected or need to restore before joining community.

We must create worlds that make time for "the life of the mind" and root them in kinship. Congressperson Maxine Waters, or Auntie Maxine, so eloquently reminds us that there are multitudinous ways to "reclaim our time"; we have the power to reclaim what is ours. In doing so, she calls us to enthusiastically reject the untruths, half-truths, and deceptions of the settler state and share our story, our dreams, and our visions. We want our way of being and becoming to be available to offer potential trajectories of Black flourishing. So, I invite you to indulge in alternative ways to tell time and to time travel. You might consider the African way, the Native way, the Māori way, or make your own way like jazz music does.

Whatever you decide, let us create a container together that allows for multiple truths, possibilities, inclinations, experiences, and relationships.

Loyal to the Soil: Place Is Horizontal

Ghetto Report Card is one of my favorite albums. Prolific rapper Earl Tywone Stevens Sr., more affectionately known as E-40, 40 Water, or E Fonzarelli, taught me several important life lessons in twenty-two songs. Chief among them is to always be loyal to your soil and, of course, that Jesus had dreads (so shake 'em). E-40 is from a small city in the Bay Area called Vallejo, a city that is largely forgotten and lives in the shadows of San Francisco and Oakland. Vallejo is home to many working-class Black residents and has suffered from poverty and poverty-related issues. Like so many Black men living in the hood, E-40 understood that his condition and circumstances, while unfair and often dangerous, don't define the place. He knew he had agency to tell his story and to offer alternative perspectives on his experience. Despite the harsh conditions, the soil turned out to provide the conditions for him to grow and multiply.

In his song "Yay Area," he offers an anthem to the dispossessed, with call-and-response choruses to make sure he is heard. He tells us he's loyal to the soil, keeps blessing oil on him, and keeps company with felons (sounds a lot like Jesus to me). This always stuck with me. I hated where I grew up; I felt mistreated, excluded, erased, and unloved, but this song reminded me that the land helped me flourish, even if that land felt like concrete. Vallejo and Apple Valley are very different but, in many ways, they shared a defining similarity in being anti-Black. I was reminded that I would not be who I am (for better or worse) without the land. The land is more than the ground for the people who occupy it; it is the relationships with humans and nonhumans, the flora and fauna, the sun, and even the air we breathe.

Yet, the soil can be poisoned. It's impossible to ignore the misogyny in some of E-40's lyrics. Some, especially people from Vallejo, might suggest that he is just a hood griot reflecting the culture of the time and place. While this might be true, the often repulsive and damaging language woven through the songs cannot be overlooked. More to the point, good or benign intentions are no answer to the harm created. That the lyrics sometimes deny my humanity as a Black woman for word play or storytelling purposes, which results in outright degradation, must be acknowledged and repaired. The fact that I learned a lot from an album that is misogynistic highlights the tension we all encounter when we reclaim parts of ourselves and our past.

There is tension in all good things. Grapes are crushed for wine, diamonds are formed under pressure, and seeds germinate in darkness—these experiences involve tension and they are signals of transformation and transmutation. None of us is just one thing, or without a past, or context.

For Black Americans, particularly ones living outside of our realm of care, it is miraculous that despite how badly America has treated us, some elements of our home languages traveled with the kidnapped hostages of enslavement and remained in our bodies and imagination.

Writer Imani Perry suggests just that in her book *Prophets of the Hood*. She shares that hip hop music is a Black space that has deep roots as a poetic and political art form. True to its origin as an African oral practice, hip hop is defined by its improvision, reinvention, and innovation of music and performance traditions. Hip hop refuses the settler hegemony and the settler explanation of societal problems. By design, it is subversive in its lyrics and delivery, enmeshed with humor, rawness, and confidence. Often overlooked, though, is hip hop's prophetic message: to see, hear, and speak to those people society deems disposable and invisible. By reclaiming embodied African ways, hip hop offers us new ground on which to think about the possibilities and promises of the future.

Poetry and its sibling hip hop offer us places of possibility within ourselves that are dark because they are ancient and hidden. Audre Lorde suggests that our creative and powerful selves survived and have grown strong through darkness, otherwise known as the unexamined reflection and feeling. In true poetic form, Lorde shares in "Poetry Is Not a Luxury" that soil for power to create resides "within each of us [and it] is neither white nor surface; it is dark, it is ancient, and it is deep."

With firm grounding and orientation, we can create anew. Seeds, wildlife, and humans—we all grow best on fecund and fertile ground.

Rootedness and Reclamation: Sacred and Sanctuary

We desire to bequeath two things to our children; the first one is roots, the other one is wings.
—SUDANESE PROVERB

Knowledge is like a garden: If it is not cultivated, it cannot be harvested.
—AFRICAN PROVERB

Rootedness in the African context suggests deep germination and growth. It is a particular way of being in concert and connected with the wilderness and wildness. Consciously and subconsciously, we reclaim things that give us vision, voice, and value. *Reclamation*, as we've discussed, is rediscovery and reconnection. Together, rootedness and reclamation sustain life of all forms. This movement of rootedness is both mystical and methodical. It is a labor without payment or acknowledgment but holds the highest value.

Our bodies, minds, and spirits are rooted somewhere. The work we have to do is to locate it and evaluate if the roots are in healthy and spacious soil so they can grow. In the current context of widespread ongoing settler colonialism, we experience restrictions on our growth, but that should not deter us. Instead, we should turn to our deep-rooted tenderness and care for ourselves and others. This tenderness and care keep us connected to each other and our responsibilities; they create art and poetry, spark activism, and give meaning to our lives.

This place is a sanctuary and the time is sacred. The word *sanctuary* has roots in the word *sanctorium*, which means a repository for holy things, or to make things whole. Making space for the most holy often means abandoning harmful ways of being and doing. It means making a distinction between where you are and where you will be, what you will accept and what you demand. It is recognizing your gifts as necessary and lifegiving and nonnegotiable. You will not make yourself smaller nor will you hide your Blackness, gayness, disabledness, or other beauty. In fact, it is those gifts that will guide you to identifying your kith and kin.

Let's sow new relations and claim our harvest.

The Weight of Being Well

"Are you sure, sweetheart, that you want to be well?" This question, which Minnie Ransom, the spirit healer, asks in Toni Cade Bambara's *The Salt Eaters*, is haunting. If we, as individuals and communities, want to be well, we must confront our insecurities, demons, and ghosts. Bambara calls us to gather the ghosts, to experience the past, and to engage with it and savor the flavor. Bambara reminds the reader, "There is a lot of weight to being well" and "Being well is no trifflin' matter." *The Salt Eaters* is set in a fictional place in the American South; the story is intentional in its nonlinear nature and in its exploration of sacred space and time from the African perspective. Bambara, like me, is improvisational. Tangents *aren't* really tangents; they are seeds and flavor agents to add texture to the main story. Poetically, *The Salt Eaters* requires the reader to treat, in literal and figurative terms, the whole self rather than parts of it. Both experimental and political in tone, Bambara's main idea is that for Black people, preserving their identity is a path to freedom and protection from the settler madness. By allowing Blackness to be our center, our home, and our kin—Black people can access our full power and potential.

For Bambara, and for me, courage is at the crux of wholeness and freedom. Sometimes we are so comfortable in our illness, trauma, or pain that it immobilizes our ability to imagine. To be courageous, we must be willing to stand in the unknown and stand firm in uncomfortable truth. Wellness, wholeness, and subsequent kinship creation require perpetual and ongoing effort. This book requires the reader to explore wellness and to pay attention to struggles, dilemmas, and relationships. I hope you take time with this text and slow down to examine carefully, and in some detail, the complexity of your own life. It is these details that force us to become more aware and that shape our behavior and energies.

Personal and political liberation is first and foremost about the liberation of the self. Reality is our collective capacity to remain grounded in our history and our spiritual traditions. True politics are not ideologies to discuss, but attitudes about your relationship with the world, which you enact daily. To thrive in spite of the settler society, we must recognize that not all power to change is man-made: that there is *divine* presence, imminence, or movements of nature that give us power. This kind of power is metaphysical and outside of material explanation. Black and African people have a tradition of spirit healing, often created from the truth and knowledge of friends, neighbors, and relatives. This connection is an affirmation of our people's power to persist and heal by bringing ourselves back to our center.

CREATION STORIES:
STORYTELLING FOR SURVIVAL

Our forefathers weren't the Pilgrims. We didn't land on Plymouth Rock. The rock was landed on us.
—MALCOLM X, "The Ballot or the Bullet" speech, April 1964

All creation stories tell of a new people for a new world.
—PATTY KRAWEC, writer and activist

In her poem "Paul Robeson," poet Gwendolyn Brooks remembers the legacy and power of singer, actor, athlete, and activist Paul Robeson. She famously writes, "we are each other's / harvest . . .we are each other's / magnitude and bond." Yet there's so much more to the poem than the reclaimed version of ubuntu and the beautiful allegory that helps us visualize our interconnectedness. Earlier in the poem Brooks celebrates the voice and power of Robeson to tell our story as Black people living under racism, fascism, and exploitation. She is calling us to recall our bounty in kinship and mutual participation in telling our collective story.

These collective stories are often relayed as creation stories—myths used to explain the creation of the world and the roles of the people in it. The settler way of life is marked by elimination, exploitation, and replacement. Relatedly, the settler myth of creating civilization in "discovered" lands is a keystone in the settler creation story. But we, Black people, have known better. Muslim minister and human rights activist Malcolm X was always steadfast in reclaiming Black people's lived experience and poetically rejecting the stories offered by settlers. In a speech he gave in April of 1964 known as "The Ballot or the Bullet" he professed, "We didn't land on Plymouth Rock. The rock was landed on us." When considering stories from Columbus to Thanksgiving, more and more Americans are rejecting the settler story and seeking alternatives. For Black and Indigenous people to achieve connection and kinship, we must continue to define ourselves for ourselves.

I believe Africans are storytellers. All over the continent we have distinct and unique ways to share the story of our collective origin or birth as a people. Africans around the world, even those disconnected from their heritage, survived by sharing creation stories. Prior to settler colonization of Africa, many West Africans believed in an animated universe, in a process of generation and recycling of energy. As a result, many of the West African creation stories focus on significant environmental and spiritual events. Complementary to Mbiti's perception of time, this understanding of our collective existence and origin offers a distinct perspective on the creation story.

Scholar and Anishinaabe writer Patty Krawec offers insightful perspective on creation stories in her book *Becoming Kin*. She crisply identifies that creation stories depend on the focal point or, as she suggests, "sometimes the center is created simply through the act of revolving around it." This book that you are reading is, in many ways, my offering of a creation story for African people around the globe—that we may become new people in a new world, where we are not on the outside of humanity but at the center.

Indigenous creation stories worldwide share some key similarities. First, the purpose of a creation story is to serve as a genealogy of a group of people, a kind of oral history of a group's existence before and after humanity. Second, these narratives offer groups of people a shared worldview that embeds important information about the land, animals, and spirits, and the values, customs, and culture of that place. Third, these stories employ imagery and allegories; these stories are told in a way to be easy to remember. Sometimes these stories are shared through dance, song, and paintings or at bedtime, around a campfire, or at special events—all with the intention of connecting deeply with people. Tactically, these stories can serve as tips or memory aids for survival and navigation along routes. Finally, creation stories offer intergenerational knowledge about identity, beliefs, and behaviors, while allowing individuals agency for interpretation.

Creation stories, poetry, and fiction share central similarities—the listener/reader is required to listen, pay attention, make connections, and search. Look for meaning in benign words and ideas, look for symbolism in the everyday, look at the text (and the world) with wonder. Why did Toni Morrison name the main character Sethe in *Beloved*? or How does the vivid description of the food impact the feeling of the meal? Great fiction, like great poems, speaks to us with profound resonance because it invites our own truths onto the landscape of their metaphors—always a little mysterious, a little malleable to the searching mind, yet sharp, clarifying, vivifying.

Much like the power of a poem, creation stories can mean many different things.

For instance, an age-old story about otherness can translate in modern terms to the lived experiences of a Black gay child. These stories create space in our lives and imaginations for the quiet power of nonconformity and personal example. And yet, in sharing a creation story, we shred the settler logic of individualism and binary thinking and remind ourselves that we are not alone or without kin, living or dead. What would it look like to explore alternative ways of considering our own existence, responsibilities, and creations?

I invite you to break out of the binary. To become originators and create new life, new stories. To fertilize your path so we can all live in full bloom.

Fiction and Freedom

> *Maybe home is somewhere I'm going and have never been before.*
> —WARSAN SHIRE, poet

In an essay entitled "The Site of Memory" in the book *Inventing the Truth*, Toni Morrison exhaustively explains that the imperative is not to remember things precisely, but to create a character, or an experience, to find its origin and meaning in an impression, an association, or a concentration. She says, "If writing is thinking and discovery and selection and order and meaning, it is also awe and reverence and mystery and magic." Explicitly, employing an archaeology metaphor, Morrison goes on in the essay to suggests we can create from the fragments and remains. These remnants are the building blocks for imagination to construct the past and for people to find their source. Fiction is frequently defined as stories that are imagined and not rooted in fact or reality. For our purposes, I submit that fiction is learning through our imagination whereas nonfiction is learning through information. That said, the idea that all stories fit neatly in one of these two categories reinforces the settler belief of binaries. What was once considered fact, can over time turn out to be fiction; take for instance the idea that being gay is a choice. And fiction often can be prophetic and offer us perspective on our current and future condition. Additionally, creation stories can be a divine message from the spirit world. Supernatural messages are neither information nor imagination; rather, they are a knowing or understanding that is connected to the unseen. What and how we create can and, I would argue, should be a combination of them all.

So many people, myself included, have yet to experience the world or life as we imagined it. Somali poet Warsan Shire reminds me, as an East African woman living in America, that while I have not felt totally connected to one part of my identity, this does not mean I cannot or will not experience it. My home, as she suggests, is a journey. A journey I may need to create, or find, or wait for—but no matter what, it exists and I must pursue it.

Freedom is not an individual experience, though settler colonialism sells it that way. Like the concept of time, freedom is not linear or predictable. One of the first acts of all settler societies is to separate kin. The calculated and concerted effort to remove Black and Indigenous fathers from a family or children from parents—is a centuries old tactic. And yet, Black and Indigenous people insisted on creating and re-creating kinship. Freedom is a place, feeling, and experience that pushes us to our potential, and often it is an uncomfortable experience.

Here, within this book, I offer parables that are fictional stories I created prioritizing freedom for my kin and allowing for wide interpretation and imagination. I went outside to feel the tree's roots and the layers of bark, to listen as the branches communicated with the wind, and to watch the ants scurry up and down the tree, which reminded me of the wisdom of an elder. Someone whose experiences and advice might be taken for granted or dismissed as not scientific or empirical but whose messages are lifegiving if listened to. More than answers, I hope the parables in this book ignite questions and critique, like Why did she choose a flowering tree? Why did she describe the people who burned the village as visitors? Why explore the table metaphor? Why choose those animals? In what ways do I dismiss knowledge that is African or Indigenous?

The underestimated, underexamined, and often dismissed role of fiction, prophecy, and revelation has relegated those who employ these approaches to the margins, and often their approaches for design and creation are not taken seriously. The very process of reflecting on how things came to be requires great courage. To risk defying the status quo and then articulate the unseen and unheard is treacherous territory in settler society. And precisely for this reason, we must encourage children and ourselves to nurse our innate propensity to tell stories and share our vision. The act of creating imaginative activities helps all of us consider alternative endings and experience them as attainable.

Kindred Archivists

> *We are born and have our being in a place of memory. We chart our lives by everything we remember from the mundane moment to the majestic. We know ourselves through the art and act of remembering.*
> —bell hooks, *Belonging: A Culture of Place*

> *It is essential to resist the depiction of history as the work of heroic individuals in order for people today to recognize their potential agency as a part of an ever-expanding community of struggle.*
> —ANGELA Y. DAVIS, activist and writer

Memory makes time and place. Archiving is a means of unforgetting and cherishing memories. To simply exist is radical. Archiving is not recording the past but instead it is an act of communing with our kin and profound worldmaking. Archiving is an invitation to just be as you choose.

Creating and then accessing public records are popular settler ways of archiving information and learning about the past, respectively. On their face, public records appear to be factual accounts of life events like birth, marriage, and death. But if you are Black in America, you know that the settler state produces these records based on their own values at the time the files were created. In my family, this became loudly apparent when we were researching my husband's family's ancestry. Even with the help of technology, professional archival researchers, and personal trips to the family hometown of Birmingham, Alabama, we were not able to learn much about his ancestors. Public records did not account for defining events in his family because, of course, such records were not kept reliably for Black people born in America. There was no record of his grandmother's adoption, his paternal great-grandmother's marriage to a white man, or any other life events that would otherwise appear. Only through context clues and oral accounts of elders who stayed in the respective cities where my husband's relatives lived were we able to learn the difficult truth of intergenerational white violence inflicted on his ancestors.

History as told by the settlers is fraught with inaccuracies and bold-faced lies. In Part I, I offered a few experimental approaches to re-membering, unforgetting, or recalling the past that does not rely on "history." However, powerful and accessible practices allow us to reclaim the past as it is happening, particularly in the form of archives, artifacts, and art. Reclaiming the art and science of self-archiving is the act of claiming our own story, knowledge, and memories. Kindred archiving, I submit, is more than selected preserved documents or records; these items are the pieces of us that tell our story. Archiving gives us windows into our personal and collective lives. Scrapbooks, vision boards, journals, recordings—all of these memories with your spirit are embedded and can be shared with your kin. Frequently, in African traditions, archival items can also be artifacts, like a newspaper, a drawing, or photographs. These artifacts and archives can also be art, as all three approaches are related and very similar. In essence, these carefully kept intentional items represent parts of who we are or were and tell a story that is important to us, but still open for interpretation and conversation. In reclaiming your own archives, you contribute to a genealogy of a world free from erasure, exploitation, and violence. More than an ancestral family tree, this kind of genealogy shares the stories of people, land, ecosystems, movements, and contexts that remember those who are no longer with us.

Archiving is both a ritual and ceremony for Black people, lending it direct connection to the spirit world. At an intimately personal level, archiving has profound influence on our ability to manifest and envision ourselves.

So be it; see to it! So be it; see to it!

Octavia Butler knew those prescient words would change her life. But who knew these words would change my life too? In viewing her archives at Huntington Library, I was magnetically attracted to Butler's spiral notebook with those words scribbled at the bottom. Butler maintained a writing routine that became ritual. She wrote not just for her readers but for herself. A seemingly insignificant archive was a loud reminder to me that whatever I choose to bring attention and consciousness to I have the power to change and create. This notebook turned out to prove Butler's belief in words, rituals, and conscious action. She manifested the dreams she outlined in that notebook. More than that, I felt a kinship in our shared experience as underestimated Black women. The beauty of archiving is that it can provide value in the present tense, both as a spiritual ritual and as a reminder of who we are and who want to become.

In my community of South Los Angeles, the Black Image Center is an organization reclaiming archiving as an emancipatory practice. This group of Black image makers, storytellers, and creatives in Los Angeles are motivated by the idea that there is a specific power that comes from telling your own story. Their Black Family Archive celebrates the power and dignity of holding space for memory, legacy, and family through archiving and digitizing old family photos. The act of preserving memories is arguably just as valuable as the preserved memories themselves. Through the Black Family Archive, Black people are able to spend sacred time considering those who came before, learning about their neighbors' families, and building stronger connections as a result.

The process of re-membering (or unforgetting), refusing (or resisting) and reclaiming (or recovering) is not just for those suffering under settler colonialism; it is also for those benefiting from the settler state. As you can tell by now, I have made a conscious choice not to address the needs and curiosities of whiteness and capitalism. By explicit design, my focus is on my African and Black relatives and that is compatible with my desire to create a safe and caring home. In navigating the tension and discomfort of settler colonialism, we are directed to a different path. One where ongoing harm as result of injustices and exploitation is stopped, acknowledged, and addressed, and we return to the strength of our collective humanity.

Promiscuous Care

> *Love takes off the masks that we fear we cannot live without and know we cannot live within. I use the word "love" here not merely in the personal sense but as a state of being, or a state of grace—not in the infantile American sense of being made happy but in the tough and universal sense of quest and daring and growth.*
>
> —JAMES BALDWIN, writer; in *The Fire Next Time*

When I think of the experiences that have inspired me to love or grieve, or that have driven me to act, those stories always involve people, places, or objects that I deeply care about. Care, deceptively, is the only thing a system cannot produce. Creating kinship with human and nonhuman creatures indiscriminately is *promiscuous care*. Coined by the writers of the *Care Manifesto*, this kind of care broadens our circle by expanding the notion of kinship. With the foundation of a caring society, we can build the infrastructures necessary for diverse kinds of care within our world. For nonhumans and humans alike, we depend on networks and systems, animate and inanimate, for our survival and well-being.

Promiscuous care calls on us to accept our interdependencies as peoples and species on this planet. Xenophobia and other forms of oppression center on the idea that care is for people who are of the same mindset or family. Capitalism puts a price on how much care is worth. In many cases, settler society treats and pays caring professionals very little. In other cases, settler institutions charge unwell, elderly, and vulnerable people exorbitant amounts for care in hospitals. By design, capitalism and colonialism cannot care. To do so would break the mechanics of their operation and proliferation.

To embrace a revolutionary culture of care requires the collective to abandon neglect and embrace connection. African studies scholar Mariamba Ani characterized the settler *asili*, developmental germ/seed of a culture, as dominated by the concepts of separation and control. This settler imposition of their values has destroyed cultures and languages all around the world in the name of progress. Robin D. G. Kelley often suggests that insurgent social movements imagined a revolutionary culture of care that not only met basic needs but eliminated oppression. The people who created these movements were often artists, activists, and neighbors who practiced a radical culture of collective care, mutual aid, community control, and the transformative power of art and politics.

Caring by way of sharing is a way of life—an attitude, a practice, and a culture—for most Black people. Caring by way of mutual aid and sustainability is a similar set of experiences for Black people around the world. This is evidenced, for instance, by how Ethiopians eat meals, offer remittances from the diaspora to relatives on the continent, and how we show love. It is rooted in a collective sense of responsibility that is cultivated from birth. From how to show up at *lexos* (mourning rituals) to how we understand hospitality as a spiritual gift between people—we are shown, more than told, what the expectation of care is for our people. We are all capable of this kind of care, Black and non-Black people, but it requires attention and intention. By widening our circles of care and ideas on kinship, we create the spiritual and physical space for an alternative, more ubiquitous care.

Former Mayor of Stockton, Michael Tubbs, has created promiscuous care and new worlds within local government. In 2019, as the youngest mayor of a large city, he created a pilot program called Universal Basic Income (UBI), which gave randomly selected residents $500 per month for two years with no strings attached. This audacious unconditional cash transfer has transformed recipients' lives. Some were able to pay off outstanding bills, purchase necessities such as food, or catch up on rent to avoid eviction. Most recipients reported a decrease in anxiety, depression, and extreme financial strain, which in turn increased their capacity for goal setting and coping with unexpected changes.

More than the material and mental health impacts, UBI reminds all of us that human value is not tied to what we do but rather who we are—relatives that require care and concern. This pilot does what kindred creation calls us to do. It offers more than a critique on the current ideology and hegemony of structural carelessness; it replaces it with a life-giving alternative. For Black and African people this is the idea of *Ujamaa*, a kind of "familyhood" or cooperative economics, in practice. From UBI, to remittances from Africans in the diaspora to their homelands, to the hood coming together to send a young person to college—these are everyday ways we can unconditionally support one another and create new worlds.

In *As We Have Always Done: Indigenous Freedom through Radical Resistance*, Mississauga Nishnaabeg scholar Leanne Betasamosake Simpson encourages Indigenous people to "join together in a rebellion of love, persistence, commitment, and profound caring and create constellations of coresistance, working together toward a radical alternative present based on deep reciprocity and the gorgeous generative refusal of colonial recognition." This transformation presents the possibility of right relations. We create the conditions for human and nonhuman dignity to be affirmed when we start from a position of care and allow being cared for.

Caring for kin is something most people accept as natural, especially the care involved in the parent-child relationship. To be a Black person has always felt like village parenting. When I am in the presence of children, I feel responsible for their safety and well-being. I learned this from my family and neighbors in how I was cared for, and it has become an embodied practice. Whether I was in the grocery store on my block or at school, I felt other Black parents cared for me and were invested in my safety and well-being. And yet, that same care can teach people to assimilate for safety and self-preservation. I think about my elders offering what they believed was "caring" advice on how to interact with the police when pulled over. I understand that ensuring my safety was their primary goal in those situations, but the kind of myopic care they offered reaffirms the system's status quo. I believe that we must tell our children the truth about the history and context of policing while also offering tools to keep them safe despite a fundamental difference in how we approach situations. Caring advice is best understood when there is a relationship or reciprocity.

bell hooks distinctively highlights the idea that love and abuse cannot coexist; I would argue that neither can care and abuse. A caring relationship can and should change when abuse or harm occurs; that's not to say care goes away altogether, but it must change so that repair and reconciliation are possible. In the words of singer Nina Simone, you have to get up from the table when love is not on the menu.

As we envision possibilities for ourselves, our relations, and our planet, let us pursue care. Let us care wildly and ambitiously so that it is an embodied way of being for generations to come.

KINDRED CREATION: FORM, FUNCTION, AND (MOST IMPORTANTLY) FREEDOM

Wherever something stands, something else will stand beside it.
—IGBO PROVERB

All ethical relationships are expressed in kinship terms. Broadening kinship means providing greater and deeper care for all things. Someone who creates with kindred creation is defined by their ability to care for relatives and engage in reciprocity. Relatives include our land, language, and lifestyle. Caring should be at the center of all roles and responsibilities—human and nonhuman alike. Kindred creation allows us to honor a connection through time, space, place, and circumstance for all things. So, to me, the role of creator is to manifest care much like the role of a poet, an organizer, or a parent.

Whether it is architecture or landscaping, art or altars—how we create is powerful and significant because we have the potential to speak to our soul. But design and creation as performed by the settler is banal at best. Reclaiming the role of creation to speak to our souls and build connection is an arduous and intentional task that cannot be done without care. Settler colonialism has indoctrinated people to believe that their personhood, work, and even the built environment is somehow distinct and separate from the politics and society that govern it.

I reject the gospel of the binary and its related concept—objectivity. Settler logic asks us to forget or ignore problems and separate them from their context. I refuse to compartmentalize my experience; instead, I am convicted by those experiences. *Conviction*, to me, is operating in active alignment with your values. Much like the Igbo proverb, I believe in a world of dualities, not one of binaries.

Recall Chinua Achebe's writing; he regularly weaves in the idea that many things can be true at once and, relatedly, that there is no one way to do something. In his book *Anthills of the Savannah*, Achebe writes:

> The trees had become hydra-headed bronze statues so ancient that only blunt residual features remained on their faces, like anthills surviving to tell the new grass of the savannah about last year's brush fires.

Let's revisit the tree metaphor and its symbolism. The tree is an elder or ancestor, a witness of many changes and experiences over time. The detailed description of the tree's destructive encounter with visitors helps us understand that even though much is forgotten and even damaged, it is not all lost. The anthill, the typically ignored and unnoticed labor of the smallest insects, remains to remind the grass of the past horrors and harm. Implicit here, is the understanding that burning grass doesn't destroy the ground; it makes it fertile for new growth and beginnings.

This seemingly literal passage has so much to offer us in how we consider starting anew and designing. Through the use of metaphor Achebe invites the reader to visualize and consider the landscape; in doing so, he affirms that nothing is absolute and newness is perpetually around the corner.

In reading, arguing, processing, deliberating, and working through this text, I hope you find connection to your own way of life and generate alternatives to the status quo. Kindred creation's form and function is to advance personal and interpersonal/interspecies connection and freedom. I offer to you my framework for exploring kindred creation centered on responsibility, reciprocity, and relationship. And with all lifegiving endeavors, questions and pursuits like these are more important than the answers: What responsibilities do you have to care for yourself and your relatives? What does a free (insert your name here) look, feel, smell, taste, and sound like? How do I embody ubuntu day to day?

These are all invitations to think and do differently. Questions don't exist just for you; they are for communion. Questions are the gestures of space making for others, the portals that are intentional in creating shared space and time. Questions are talismans on the adventures of nurturing difference. In the dual crisis of settler colonialism and capitalism, we are conditioned to believe we are what we produce. That results in a creation approach that prioritizes productivity and materialism. Kindred creation asks us to prioritize process and understanding—requiring presence over productivity. Our collective emancipation from settler colonialism depends on returning to ourselves—reclaiming kinship and belonging. Assert your beautiful humanity and belong wherever you are—without validation, approval, or permission. Black people being fully received by themselves will create freedom.

Let us explore this return, reception, and reclamation through three concepts introduced in part one: land, language, and lifestyle.

Recover: Land

When we love the Earth, we are able to love ourselves more fully. I believe this. The ancestors taught me it was so.
—bell hooks, *Sisters of the Yam*

We do not inherit the earth from our ancestors; we borrow it from our children.
—CHIEF SEATTLE, Native American leader

The land is our family and the waterways are our bloodline.
—QUEEN QUET, Gullah Geechee Nation

Land is a relative. It is a living, breathing organism that sustains all of us—animate and inanimate, human and nonhuman. Land, like a relative, cannot be owned. It is not a resource to be bought, sold, or exploited. Land is natural endowment, based on use, stewardship, and access, not ownership. Land is the embodiment of reciprocity. The balance of giving and receiving. To Africans, this balance is sustainability. *Ayni*, a Quechua and Aymara word for sacred reciprocity, is an ethic translated as "today for you, tomorrow for me." Reciprocity, not recognition, is the central tenet being inextricably linked to the land and to each other. The land is one of the most visible examples of our interdependence as a species.

The settler legacy of rewriting history and geography for the descendants of the Native Americans, enslaved, and formerly enslaved African people is the ongoing vicious land dislocation, dispossession, and reallocation, which is forcing them to occupy fewer and fewer space(s) in America today. In *Reclaiming Stolen Earth* writer Jawanza Eric Clark exposes the ironic reality of the Black and Indigenous relationship to the land as he observes that "[the people that] viewed the land as sacred, who argued against the privatization of land as one's personal property, and who maintained a worldview opposed to the mechanization and objectification of the land and the exploitation of its natural resources, have had land stolen from them."

For Africans and Indigenous people, the land is everything. Across the continent of Africa, land has spiritual, cultural, ecological, social, and cosmological power in the lives of inhabitants. Depriving a person of land means robbing them of their sacred personhood, being, and identity—in other words, their full humanity. In an era of intense climate change and crisis, protecting and reclaiming the land is not just a theoretical imperative but one that impacts all of our lives. The real and tangible consequences of exploiting the land have indelible impacts on agriculture, pastoralism, fishing, hunting and gathering, and other subsistence activities, including having access to water.

Belonging and stewarding are core concepts in the African understanding of the relationship between land and humans. Settlers have not only claimed ownership of land but they have evicted Black and Indigenous people from their homes. Black writer and scholar Saidiya Hartman describes her pervasive sense of dispossession in her book *Lose Your Mother: A Journey Along the Atlantic Slave Route*:

> Two people meeting on the avenue will ask, "Is this where you stay?"
> Not, "Is this your house?" "I stayed here all my life" is the reply.

Staying is living in a country without exercising any claims on its resources. It is the perilous condition of existing in a world in which you have no investments. It is having never resided in a place that you can say is yours.

I, too, use the language of *stay* and reading that passage again makes it clear to me why. Black folk understand that despite building this country and nurturing it, it still isn't ours. That we are strangers in our own house and routinely made aware that we don't belong.

Subconsciously, as a Black person living in America, I never felt a relationship to land that felt reciprocal or enduring. In recent years, I have serendipitously been connected to many Black farmers, whom I affectionately call Freedom Farmers, who grow their own food and create freedom in the context they inherited. Many of those farmers found farming as a way to meet basic needs for themselves and have since offered me metaphors and historical context for the role of land in our spiritual development and kindred relations. Food was a weapon of control by slaveholders and settlers, most often used as a means to dominate and exploit. From enslaved Africans hiding seeds in their hair, to building sisterhood with a basket of biscuits, to the Black Panther Party Breakfast Program, the story of Black food has also been a story about self-determination.

Seeds are the origin of most fresh food around the world. The small and powerful plant embryos can feed countless people and animals. Women have most often kept, chosen, and sown the seeds in African societies. Peasant women, in particular, have led the movement for seed and food sovereignty. Food and seed sovereignty are distinct ways to reclaim production, distribution, and consumption of our food systems. Seed keepers and food producers are reclaiming traditional methods of food and medicine that are better aligned with ecological processes and human health, which in turn offer us an alternative to industrial settler agriculture to create a nourishing future.

bell hooks, who is invoked heavily in this book, routinely shared wisdom about the settler version of history and how it is designed to erase and forget Black peoples' deep and long-standing connection to the land. Living in modern society, many Black people forget that we were first and foremost a

people of the land, farmers. The African perspective has a broader understanding of land as linked to being and identity. There are spiritual and
cosmological interactions between soil, rock, water, and the land. These
are inseparable connections. Land belongs to the living, the dead, and the
unborn, making it inalienable. In African spiritual traditions, communion
with the ground of the ancestors facilitates meaningful prayers to God, and
it's the departed who guide and provide for the living.

John Mbiti, who wrote extensively on African philosophy, sheds light
on how critical concepts like land are understood as references to actual
relationships. Take, for instance, the word *love*; it is a reference to the actions
that express a loving relationship. Love exists if people act lovingly. In the
African setting, social obligations and actions are more than objects and
transactions; they are relationships, kinship—the most central concept in
Black and African societies.

Like most relationships, the land tells a story—the story of a witness and
an elder. Ethnobotanist Gary Nabhan suggests that we can't meaningfully
proceed with reclamation and restoration of land without "re-story-ation."
This requires humans, and in particular settlers, to reject the idea that
humans are the pinnacle of Creation and instead understand that we must
look to the land and other species for guidance and wisdom on how to
live. By observing the ways of the flowering mimosa trees, we notice that
these teachers show us how to live above and below ground and, even more
important, how to make medicine and food from sunlight and water—all to
give freely to the world around us.

For Black people globally, reestablishing a relationship with the land
is reconciliation, care, and protection. For settlers, reconciliation is not an
imposed option. Black people and Africans must reclaim the relationship to
the land and define the conditions for a new relationship. Reconciliation is
only available if a caring relationship was first established. To put it plainly,
how can we reconcile a relationship when there was never one in the first
place? The land and the exploited inhabitants are clear that they do not
want to return to the way things were.

This kind of amicable relationship without the labor of repair is plainly
evident today in England's amnesia and delusion regarding its role in

colonization and its relationships with the colonized. In 2022, Queen Elizabeth II told the president and people of Barbados: "I look forward to the continuation of the friendship between our two countries and peoples." This comment was the Queen's response to the Barbadian people refusing to pledge allegiance to the monarch just months before she passed away from natural causes at the age of ninety-six. As the head of state of a prolific colonizing country, she refers to the centuries of colonial domination as "friendship." Rather than opting for oppressor comfort, even in their old age, we must reclaim the terms and expectations of an amicable and kindred relationship and protect the relationship from future harm.

To engage with the land as a relative is to experience interdependence. Nick Estes, Indigenous scholar and citizen of the Lower Brule Sioux Tribe, has written a great deal on the role of freedom, land, and the struggle of Indigenous people to reclaim their land and way of life. We know that water is life and that water has memory. This is not just the chant at the camps of Standing Rock, nor is it a mystical idea. Materially, all humans and countless nonhumans need water in order to stay alive. The gathering at Standing Rock represented a fight for a different relationship to land and water, one that embodies a central tenet of Oceti Sakowin philosophy: we want to live and we want our children to live, so we have to protect the water.

Restitution of land is one approach to reclaiming land. Reclaiming land does require return, but implicit in the settler restitution model is a negotiation. It often asks African and Indigenous people to participate in a process designed to be objective and transactional. These processes, therefore, are unable to account for the spiritual, cultural, and intergenerational harm they inflict, intentionally or not. These processes show limited success in places. Take for instance, the Waitangi Tribunal that resulted in rematriation of land back to the Māori people in New Zealand; that return also created the foundation for an exploitative banking and mortgage system. Reclaiming land, then, should be carefully designed outside of the settler colonial context to avoid the downstream and unintended consequences. For many Native American tribes, treaties were an approach to create understanding and outline consequences for people you do not trust. That skepticism was later validated if we reflect on the role treaties play in accelerating theft and exploitation. Whether it is returning land or creating treaties to protect land, let us reclaim the land as a sovereign relative that deserves care and reciprocity. Let us learn not to tether our reclamation to the colonial way of life and instead look to our relatives, living and transitioned, land and water, inanimate and animate—to offer us guidance.

Diébédo Francis Kéré, African architect, reclaims his Burkina Faso traditions to create the built environment in collaborative ways. In "In the Studio," an interview with writer Nana Biamah-Ofosu in *Kinfolk* magazine, Kéré names that one of the most significant damages of colonial power was "its careless extraction of resources on the continent." From his perspective, architecture "has a division between building and intellect—they [settlers] came with the structures but didn't engage with the local culture, traditional building techniques or people." A key feature to his design approach is creating a sustainable and durable building, and in doing so, offering the inhabitants a joyful and comfortable experience.

The fact that the settler vision created a design that does not serve a purpose for the Indigenous people is emblematic of the disconnect between designer and community. Kéré, however, was able to reclaim his traditional approach while remembering and reckoning with the past colonial domination. For the National Assembly in Benin, he created a building that included the canopy of a live tree at the center of the compound to provide a space for gathering and governance—this is not only a nod to the precolonial history, but it reclaims the African practice of communing with trees to make decisions.

Architecture, like most creation, documents our values on our world and its inhabitants. The African hieroglyphics of Kemet and Nubia tell the story of the people and their cultural meanings through the built environment. Kindred creation asks us to reclaim the language that tells our collective precolonial narratives.

Recover: Language

To read a poem is to hear it with our eyes; to hear it is to see it with our ears.
—OCTAVIO PAZ, poet

We must make language accountable to the truths of our experience.

—JUNE JORDAN, poet

Lullabies, spirituals, songs, signing, writing, and collages are a few varied forms of language. From artistic to abstract, these ways of communicating our thoughts tell a story. Language is the way we connect to our kin. From blues to hip hop and Geechee to Ge'ez, Black people have and continue to reclaim language in the words, arrangements, sounds, and vibrations in which we express ourselves and our realities.

Language, for Black people, is most frequently a spiritual experience, an encounter with the divine. Language is how we become aware of our consciousness, of our world. It is how we reconstruct ourselves independent of oppression. Language offers us a new reality. The reconceptualization and reconstruction of Black people must include the fundamental dissimilarity between the settler way and African people. Our genetic, cultural, and ancestral heritage as Africans in the diaspora remains no matter the social reality we are in. The separation from our homeland, whether by kidnapping or other forced migration, continues to be a kind of incarceration in the settler conception of reality.

Blues music began as the language of working and freed Black people. It is an authentic Black and African expression of humanity in the form of rhythm and movement. Black people are the blues. The blues is a living testament to the supernatural gifts to survive and thrive in defiance to anti-Blackness, settler colonialism, and capitalism. Rev. Dr. Martin Luther King Jr. eloquently describes the language of blues and jazz music and its role in communicating more creatively in his address written for the 1964 Berlin Jazz Festival in which he says:

> Jazz speaks for life. The Blues tell the story of life's difficulties . . . they take the hardest realities of life and put them into music, only to come out with some new hope or sense of triumph. This is triumphant music.

King ends with a call to action: use time and message creatively, like jazz music courageously does—not simply in tempo and cadence, but in its very insistence of existing despite the realities and rules presented. King believed that human salvation was in the hands of the creative minority of people who refused to accept injustice.

Language is *poises*, the activity of world-making or creating anew. Poetry is a distinct kind of language that is the deliberate, self-conscious crafting of the world. This is no different than the labor and love of birth—to bring something into the world that did not exist before. Poet Octavio Paz offers a lesson in his transposing of commonplace senses with activities. In this way, the metaphor is a contradiction of ordinary conventions, a kind of juxtaposition. For Paz, there is no direct or adequate language for expressing the transcendent nature of a poem. And yet indirectly, he uses language in innovative and creative ways to symbolize and communicate something that transcends representation. For those willing to think about it longer, the metaphor becomes a kind of secret language, one that intentionally flips the original nature of things and expresses their intrinsic essences. Language is an investigation, not a transaction. In this way, the extra time we spend with the text allows us to release the dominant way to reading, thinking, and knowing and reconsider all the alternative ways of understanding the statement about language being an investigation rather than a transaction. Spend a day with this statement; you may explore hundreds of examples that support or refute the idea, but either way, possibilities and revelation become apparent and abundant.

Poet June Jordan embodies the self-reflective and revelatory features of poetry and its vehicle, language. Language structures our reality. Language seeds freedom; it is the vehicle that germinates and grows self-esteem, power, and connection. With language, we can explore our world on our terms, in spite of settler society. *Poetry* is a word derived from the word *poises*, to create anew. Yet, recalling *Sankofa*, the idea that we must look back to go forward, we can't create or move forward without accounting for the past and holding it accountable—language can do this. In this way, a poetic understanding of the past becomes prophetic. I am not speaking of *prophecy* in the Western definition of the word as meaning predicting the future; instead it is distilling the meaning of the past to convey revelation. Poetry and creative expression function not just as a vehicle for connection, truth, or expression, but as being intrinsic to revelation and worldmaking.

Language is the message, the messenger, and the method. African and Indigenous philosophies understand the interconnectedness of all three to transmitting values, wisdom, and knowledge. Considering the settler context, language can and has been used for profane purposes, most perniciously in education, where language has been employed to groom and facilitate the exploitation and exclusion of oppressed peoples. Rather than use the settler language, in its form and rules, to find and construct freedom, we can explore African and Black languages that embed our unique purpose, people, and process to share knowledge, build relationships, and create anew. The Indigenous African languages being reconstructed and reconceptualized include ancient languages like Ethiopian Ge'ez as well as more modern languages like Gullah Geechee and African-American Vernacular English (AAVE).

Ge'ez loosely translates to mean "to become free." For me, exploring the foundation of Ethiopian language and writing systems has offered emancipation from the English language. Although I am not fluent in the ancient language (few people are), exploring these systems offers me the cultural affirmation that Black people have and continue to exist and thrive outside of the settler society. Ge'ez is a language that is a uniquely Indigenous intellectual tradition; in no way has it been poisoned by settlers. This intellectual tradition is the foundation for Ethiopian philosophy and education, which is grounded in kinship and community life because that is how knowledge and wisdom are shared through generations. Returning to African language systems like Ge'ez is a way to reject the settler language and return to African thought systems and philosophies.

Reconceptualizing and reclaiming African philosophy and ways of life can be done by learning Indigenous languages so we can continue cultural dissemination to close the gap so we do not experience cultural estrangement. Beyond its usage in the church, Ge'ez contributes to the development of knowledge systems in Ethiopia extending to the areas of history, law, and medicine.

Zera Yacob was an Ethiopian philosopher who wrote *Hatata* in 1667. *Hatata*, which means "inquiry," was one of the first written philosophical treatises to tackle ideas of rationalism, reason, religion, slavery, and the status of women. Long before the Enlightenment and far away from Europe and America, Yacob proposed groundbreaking ideas that were dismissed, ignored, or later coopted by settlers. In spite of those realities, Yacob used an Indigenous language to create a new way of thinking. *Zera Yacob*, in Amharic, translates to the "seed of Jacob."

By now you may notice the unintentional and intentional harvesting of metaphors of this section—from the fertile and fecund land, to the seed keepers, and now to language seeding new conceptions of self and freedom. Language can also insulate and protect people from settlers. The Gullah Geechee language and culture are true embodiments of maintaining African roots on American soil. Gullah Geechee is an Indigenous Black language in America that has direct linguistic and cultural ties to Sierra Leone. By rejecting the English language and creating a new language that incorporates elements of kin, culture, and heritage, the Gullah Geechee people have intentionally created a sacred language.

Reclaiming, remixing, and reconceptualizing reality is evident in the everyday and exceptional lives of Black people in America. On September 16, 1995, at the age of twenty-five, Tupac Amaru Shakur was murdered. Despite his young age and unjust treatment while he was alive, he was a prolific poet, a platinum selling artist, and, I believe, a philosopher and prophet. He keenly understood the power of language and how to connect with different audiences in his intentional use of AAVE. He used language, whether conscious or unconscious, in a way that is Indigenous to the African oral tradition, like boasting, toasting, tall tales, clowning, and woofing as well as keeping it real to the experiences of the hood.

If language offers us new ways to make or deepen connections and commitments or protect our way of life, then we need more than design as a practice. Without language to speak to our experiences and realities, we are unable to create sustaining lifestyles and will be trapped in the settler nightmare. The use of language functions as a way to shape our experiences and take responsibility for consciously determining and continuing the traditions of our kin.

Let us reclaim our unique and sacred ways of communicating and communing.

Recover: Lifestyle

There's nothing new under the sun,
but there are new suns.

—OCTAVIA BUTLER, epigram from unpublished *Parable of the Trickster*

First they made prayers, then they sang and they danced,
and then they made relatives.

—WANBI I MAYASLECA, artist and activist

I love being Black. Black people make everything more beautiful. Black people are deeply intentional people by nature and nurture. We express joy and delight in colorful, eccentric, and ornamental ways of being. The curves in our movement and melodies, the way we intuit and know the unknowable, our transformation of life from death-making societies—we are a sight to behold! We are the spirit moving.

The way we live, labor, love, and practice our cultures, care, and activism—all are unique and worthy of appreciation and reclamation. We create worlds of magic and joy, in the here and now, through our hair and our dance. We practice freedom and connect to Mother Africa in ways that are often subconscious. When we submit to the settler logic of binaries, we reduce our glorious existence to simplistic, superficial interactions. When the sacred and the secular are promoted to be distinct and never allowed to interact, we limit our humanity and the world around us. When this happens, our lives, as Black people, push further away from our potential and our despair deepens.

I've inherited so much from my relatives, blood and chosen kin alike. One of my many gifts is participating in an Idir/Eder, an Indigenous Ethiopian mutual aid/savings circle that, as a result, is a community-creating association. Many other African contexts have similar arrangements, like Susu in Ghana and or the Free African Society in the US.

Unsurprisingly, Eder originated in rural peasant communities within Ethiopia to raise funds for community needs including funeral costs, pensions for elders, and farming loss, as well as to coordinate free labor of members in community activities. Throughout my childhood in America, I watched and participated in the social aspects of Eder as my parents and other families came together on a monthly basis to pray, break bread, and provide support to each other. I understood by observation that Ethiopian culture and lifestyle value and embed reciprocity in all interactions, including financial and emotional support.

Many Africans born in Africa and living in America or Europe reclaim their culture, traditions, and lifestyles in their new place. Resisting assimilation to the new country and creating kin requires people to create an alternative. One alternative is to create a kind of microcommunity, organized and self-governed. These communities are the manifestations of our dreams and not a Black version of any current invention.

We, future ancestors, have so many gifts to bequeath to coming generations of Black people that are more than the "Black Wealth" or "Black Ownership" theology. Paramount among those gifts, is the ability to live to our fullest potential and power. Kindred creation is one way to consider offering that gift, by sharing the story of our past, by recognizing ourselves (and our genius), and by using our innate ingenuity to fly and create new worlds. As jazz musician Thelonious Monk says, "A genius is one who is most like him/herself." This is a reminder that who we are, as we are, is exceptional if we have the courage to be those people and not succumb to dominant ways of being.

As organisms, humans uniquely have the ever-expanding capacity for growth. Octavia Butler believed humans were organisms with intuitive instincts for self-preservation that had been honed by evolution to make them clever but mean, creative but selfish and short-sighted. She was not wrong. This self-interested disposition has led to global devastation in the form of capitalism and colonization; and it continues in the methodolatry settlers impose in design, spirituality, and science. We are left with a continuation of the settler colonial subjugation of our lifestyle.

Central to African ways of life is the presence of the spirit. Many Indigenous philosophies believe that people are spiritual beings having a human experience. The spiritual potency of our existence cannot be undervalued, undermined, or otherwise ignored. Reclaiming our lifestyle is revaluing our ways of being and imagining. It is restoring ourselves, each other, and the land through rituals, routines, and revelation. Africans have long held that revelation, like prophecy, is not what the settler definition has offered us. African spirituality tells us that the notion of revelation is one that is living, continuous, and omnipresent. The divine is able to speak to and through any being, human or nonhuman. Revelation is not exclusive to religious leaders or settlers, but all creatures have access to the spirit world by way of dreams, prayer, or communion with nature.

Reclaiming the African way of life also means reclaiming our art and artistry. It means welcoming home the poets, prophets, and seers whose life and work illuminate the deep tradition of prophetic truthtellers who have helped us understand the world better. To the settler project, colonizing the mind and spirit was, and continues to be, as important as colonizing the land. It was necessary for the settlers to not only replace spiritual systems and ways of connecting with the spirit, but to classify African spirituality using pejorative terms, suggesting it to be a kind of evil magic, mysticism, or superstition—furthering the experience of oppression and subjugation. Settler society has attempted to render African and Black spiritual modalities not rooted in Western religious formats as irrelevant, invisible, or uncivilized. Yet we know that it is the spirit that keeps us going during unthinkable conditions. Lakota artist Wanbli Mayasleca helps us visualize the first encounter between enslaved Africans and the Indigenous population of the Carolinas. Kinship for both Indigenous groups begins with prayer, followed by movement, culminating in relations or connection. African and Indigenous people know that without an invitation to the spirit and sacred connection, kinship is not possible.

I do not believe it is a coincidence that Black people in Watts, California, pour out liquor to remember "the dead homies" and that West Africans do the same to honor ancestors in libation ceremonies. Not only are they connecting with the ancestors in traditional ways but we, as Black people, are honoring the natural spaces and land where those people could be remembered. Through this ritual and ceremony, Black Americans and Africans can connect and communicate with transitioned kin and their spirits.

Often in Native American spirituality land and location are revered as sacred places where ceremonies to connect with spirits are conducted. Similarly, today in the dwellings of Black people around the world, you can find an altar, much like the altars created in Africa for centuries. Though not identical, you can find your own places or ways to commune with the spirit/God/Creator, to receive spiritual, mental, and emotional comfort, to preserve the memory of a loved one, or to gain inner guidance. Sometimes that communing looks like an airbrushed t-shirt with the image of a loved one superimposed on a serene background, or it's in a formal living room with framed photos, candles, a lace tablecloth, and flowers. No matter what its arrangement, its purpose remains to offer us connection to kin, living and transitioned, and to be a physical place of refuge.

The conversation between living creatures, spirits, and God/divine/Creator is a defining feature of the African and the kindred creation design framework. Without honoring that which cannot be seen or acknowledged in the physical world, design is a method or series of routine activities. I submit to you that revelation and intuition are the cornerstones of kindred creation. In their article "Educating African-Centered Psychologists," African-centered psychology scholars Erylene Piper-Mandy and Taasogle Daryl Rowe propose a framework that outlines the seven moments that define the lives of humans that then end in the journey of the spirit:

> These frame the arc, sweep or path of a human spirit—Before, Beginning, Belonging, Being, Becoming, Beholding, and Beyond; the path is cyclical and four dimensional. The seven moments refer to periods of articulation of human spirit: the path of the Spirit.

This buried and underused framework was groundbreaking to me. Although I can't be sure how it was created, I am sure about how I discovered it in the heaps of online research I conducted to learn more about African-centered philosophy and theology—and divine direction. I followed tangents, took breaks, and returned with a new direction—in that time the spirit directed me to read this paper to the end, which is where I read these few revelatory sentences.

African-centered psychology is a discipline that offers Black people globally new ways to consider themselves, their families, and their worldview. Wade Nobles, a scholar and pioneer of African-centered philosophy, reminds Black people that the ability to define ourselves and our kin is the most important element of human beingness, and to reach full possibility and unlimited potentiality, the human spirit must be whole, which he defines as confident, competent, and conscious. Along with the spirit, an important principle that distinguishes various African cultures from Western and settler cultures is Africans cultures' intuitive relationship and harmonization between humans and nature.

Recalling "The Parable of the Tree" in Part I, notice how settlers attempt to control and understand nature in scientific and technological terms. This kind of thinking separates nature from humans and creates the conditions for carelessness and destruction. When we reclaim our wisdom, this includes reclaiming our understanding of science independent of colonization and capitalism. This means appreciating light for its kaleidoscopic abilities and iridescent colors, not just for its mathematical obedience. When we allow the spirit to lead the discovery and design, we experience a healing or a joyful connection to, or kinship with, our world.

No matter what path we choose—Black or African or other Indigenous way of life—reclaiming our lifestyles is how we connect and create our families, communities, and nations. When we follow our embodied and spiritual ways, we become ungovernable to the colonial state and opt into our own world.

Though I am not religious, I have long held embodied spiritual practices, another gift shared with me by my mother and grandmothers. They showed me the rituals and routines of Ethiopian spiritual traditions. I learned to fast for Tsom and burn incense to cleanse a room. I learned to pray before every important activity and pray in community to reach the saints and God. I learned that an intentional life is the only life worth living, and that our homes, lifestyle, and culture must invite the spirit in to do the unimaginable.

There is no (kindred) creation without the divine. The spirit always has her hand in the memorable, majestic, medicinal, magical, and miraculous creation.

MYTHS, MAPS, AND METAPHORS

Maps are only as significant as the journey one takes with them. Maps can show us powerful patterns or steward critical shared resources. In the case of the Bozo fishing people of the Niger River basin in Mali, maps showed people the surface and underground flow of water, allowing them to control this vital resource. At the start of each new year, elders assemble the children of their community in a public place to demonstrate how their ancestor, Maroro, learned about the properties and creative powers of water. In this outdoor classroom of sorts, the children draw graphic signs on the ground representing different types of water and learn about their nature and linkages with each other. The process of mapmaking is as important as the knowledge conveyed in the map itself. At one point in the ritual reenactment, each child stands on the sign that the elder believes corresponded to their character. This gesture signified that the waters of today's world and future worlds will be controlled by people.

Another kind of mapping in some African societies is one that employs visual and tactile aids to help visualize metaphors. Ethiopians often use objects, artifacts, and even physical inscriptions to retell myths and other stories of historical and cultural importance. Similarly, among the Tabwa of southeastern Democratic Republic of Congo, the migration path of mythical ancestral heroes is inscribed in the skin of initiates to the Butwa society.

Toni Morrison reminds us that our myths, Black and African, hold the seeds to new life and that stories and songs offer us hidden (and sometimes subconscious) messages for these new lives. Maps, myths, and metaphors are social constructions whose form, content, and meaning vary with the intentions of their makers. Whether in the arrangement of beads and shells on a *lukasa* or in the tie-dyed cloth of Barnum, the process of selecting, omitting, and positioning is influenced by the maker's desire to influence specific social and political situations. This intentional selection means that the sign systems employed do not necessarily have to be understood by everyone. They may be esoteric and therefore understood by only a small group, or they may speak to a much wider audience. It is this variable and changing social nature that exemplified the African worldmaking traditions.

Maps, metaphors, and myths can be informative and beautiful, but they are no substitute for the labor of meaning making for ourselves. We must explore and look for patterns in our lives and in the world, understanding that patterns only reveal themselves when we care and create. Mvskoke poet Joy Harjo's poem "A Map to the Next World" invites us to create our own maps. She ends the poem by naming the reality that humans were never perfect, but together the journey is perfect. She acknowledges we will make mistakes; in fact, we might make the same mistakes over and over again, but "You must make your own map."

MY OFFERING: LET'S MAKE RELATIVES AND BEGIN AGAIN

Alternative Endings and Radical Beginnings

Tell no lies, claim no easy victories.
—AMÍLCAR CABRAL, engineer, political organizer, and diplomat; from *National Liberation and Culture*

After all, a person is herself, and others. Relationships chisel the final shape of one's being. I am me, and you.
—N. K. JEMISIN, *The Fifth Season*

From the womb to the tomb, that's one trip that we all take. We all lead circular lives. Life to death, and the lives we create in between take unpredictable paths.

Our paths are much like the web of a spider—formed as a circle and invisible to the unexamined view, they bring us back to the beginning to connect and continue. A new or alternative way forward requires an invitation to our feelings and the spirit. Poetry and prayer, or communing with divine forces, offer consciousness to discover or invent new ways of being. I did not write this alone. From conception to completion, this text required two heartbeats. It also required a conversation with many ancestors, elders, and children. That is because all knowledge is produced through relationship.

For me, knowledge is produced when I'm communing with nature or with other books. However you decide to create new knowledge, be sure to consider your kin, living and transitioned. I was pregnant with my first child when I began sharing my decolonization journey; I carried her in and outside the womb as I created new frameworks and wrote articles to offer alternatives to the status quo. While carrying my second child, wrapped on my chest, I completed this text and pushed myself to think beyond decolonization. Now, while pregnant with my third, this book is heading to publication.

As in birth, let us participate and honor the process of gestation and make room for what is new and alternatives that are growing. And like birth, let's keep it real. Birthing anything brings you to the edge of death; it pushes you to you limits and very rarely comes effortlessly. Pan-African poet and philosopher Amílcar Cabral makes that wisdom practical; we must be honest about our difficulties, mistakes, and failures so that people understand the reality of this labor. Creating new relatives and birthing new life will not be easy or quick; in fact, this sacred work never ends. Returning to *The Salt Eaters*, let's recall that the ongoing project of reclaiming African knowledge is reflective of African people. From our jazz-inflected rhythms, lyrical language, prophecies, improvisational digressions, and seemingly tangential stories, I hope you are called to widen your circle of care and dare to connect to others, human and nonhuman.

Long before I gave birth to my children and this book, I dedicated my life to revolutionary mothering and birthing justice. I am eternally grateful for the many ancestors that guided me as I labored to birth and deliver this text. We create alternative endings and radical beginnings when we decide to reconstruct our authentic self. You've met some of my family, kinfolk, and neighbors—some of whom are nonhuman. We've looked to the past to relive the death and rage that is a byproduct of enslavement and settler colonization, as well as to recover lost wisdom and rootedness in African ways. Through my lived experience and personal connections, I've shared what has inspired and influenced me on my journey. I hope this reading has offered more questions than answers; that this is your invitation to think, write, and create in Indigenous ways.

As we end, or begin again, I want to offer you some affirmations:

I claim that together we will embody a routine and easy acceptance of signs and spirits.

I claim that we will embrace ourselves and our families, past and present.

I claim that we will celebrate our distinct way of knowing and being.

I claim that we will create rather than consume.

I claim that we will tell our embodied truths and resurrect the memories of those destroyed and exploited.

I claim we will birth new worlds and save the one we inhabit.

So be it; see to it!

Parable of the Traveler

Free people, free land.

Proper posture, pointe shoes, and a pulled-up bun. And, of course, tutu and tights, the uniform of her tribe. Her movements were rehearsed and routine. She twirled to sounds unfamiliar in a culture and context that sucked the vitality of her people. Living between many worlds, always in tension, kept her distracted from her gifts.

Zuriya's dancing was magic in movement. It gave her international notoriety and visibility, but not on her terms. She performed on stages that were sterile and pristine with audiences that loved her performing but not her as a person.

She grew up in the hunnids. It was there that she fell in love with movement, shapeshifting, and time travel. As a child, she witnessed the improvisational, free-flowing, spiritual movements of Turf dancing. Few people outside of her community truly understood its meaning and how the Turf dancers brought down the clouds to dance. Even fewer people knew that, before ballet, she was first a Turf dancer. She practiced at the corner of E. 14th almost daily, that is until her best friend Kebir was violently taken away. She tried to continue in tribute to him and to express her profound grief, but it wasn't long until she decided to pursue a dance that would take her around the world.

Ashes to ashes, dust to dust—a circular movement. They want us to believe that we arrive and depart alone, but she knew better. She just knew. In her body, mind, and spirit—she knew.

Dust always seems to follow her anywhere she goes. The fine particles of the Earth can be stuck to a person, can accumulate on the ground or be suspended in the air. Dust reminds us that no matter how hard we try or how long we wash, we are connected to the Earth and each other. Dust is special and shapeshifting to those who know this. It has a kind of magical movement, traversing space and time.

Her travels took her to Europe and on charity trips to Africa. It was there that she felt the connection between East Africa and East Oakland, between Ekitaguriro and Turf dancing. Maybe it was from twirling or maybe it was the movement, looking inward. Whatever it was, she knew rotations and circular movements are meditative, and as with all emancipatory endeavors, she began asking questions. Questions that hurt, that exposed, and ones that burned—questions like, Why does society value ballet more than Turf dancing? Who am I performing for? Does it make me feel alive or connected? These questions caused a different kind of movement, one of reflection, connection, and responsibility toward her kin.

Without a map or end destination, she chose not to fix the world she inherited. Instead, she chose to time travel. To stand at the corner where she grew up and invite Kebir back from the spirit world. He told her about the many universes he encountered and his greatest lesson—that the truth lies where metaphors turn to prophecy. Then, she had a revelation, the seed and Samaritan have one thing in common—the generational power of a parable. The seed traveled through the dark soil to proliferate and the Samaritan refused to be a bystander to violence and, instead, acted with care.

Following that supernatural encounter, she continued her journey inward. There she found fullness and beauty. Her journey also led her to her people, her kin—those who also travel with creation and the divine.

That which is good is never finished.

—AFRICAN PROVERB

KEY READINGS

Anderson, Kim. "Affirmations of an Indigenous Feminist." In *Indigenous Women and Feminism: Politics, Activism, Culture*, eds. Cheryl Suzack, Shari M. Huhndorf, Jeanne Perreault, and Jean Barman. Chicago: University of Chicago Press, 2010.

Ani, Marimba. *Yurugu: An African-Centered Critique of European Cultural Thought and Behavior*. Trenton, NJ: Africa Research and Publications, 1994.

Bambara, Toni Cade. *The Salt Eaters*. London: Penguin Classics, 2021.

Biamah-Ofosu, Nana. "Into the Studio: Diébédo Francis Kéré." *Kinfolk* no. 41, September 7, 2021. https://www.kinfolk.com/diebedo-francis-kere/.

Brooks, Gwendolyn. "Paul Robeson." In *The Essential Gwendolyn Brooks*. New York: Library of America, 2005.

The Care Collective. *The Care Manifesto: The Politics of Compassion*. London: Verso Books, 2020.

Cordova, V. F., and Kathleen Moore, Kurt Peters, Ted Jojola, and Ambe Lacy (eds.). *How It Is: The Native American Philosophy of V. F. Cordova*. Tucson: University of Arizona Press, 2007.

Davis, Angela Y., Gina Dent, Erica R. Meiners, and Beth E. Richie. *Abolition. Feminism. Now.* Chicago: Haymarket Books, 2022.

Harjo, Joy. "A Map to the Next World." In *How We Became Human: New and Selected Poems: 1975–2001. New York: W. W. Norton, 2004*.

Hartman, Saidiya. *Lose Your Mother: A Journey along the Atlantic Slave Route*. New York: Farrar, Straus and Giroux, 2008.

hooks, bell. *Teaching to Transgress*. London: Routledge, 2014.

Hopkins, Pauline E. *One Blood*. London: X Press, 1996.

Jordan, June, Lauren Muller, and The Blueprint Collective, eds. *June Jordan's Poetry for the People*. London: Routledge, 1995.

King, Martin Luther, Jr. "On the Importance of Jazz." Opening Address written for the 1964 Berlin Jazz Festival, September 1964.

Lorde, Audre. "Poetry Is Not a Luxury." In *Teaching Black: The Craft of Teaching on Black Life and Literature*, eds. Ana-Maurine Lara and drea brown. Pittsburgh: University of Pittsburgh Press, 2021, 125–27.

Monk, Thelonious. "T. Monk's Advice." Document transcribed by Steve Lacy, 1960. Quoted in Tom Taylor, "Thelonious Monk's 25 Handwritten Tips for Musicians," *Far Out*, September 2, 2021, https://faroutmagazine.co.uk /thelonious-monk-25-handwritten-tips-for-musicians/.

Moraga, Cherríe, and Gloria E. Anzaldúa, eds. *This Bridge Called My Back: Writings by Radical Women of Color*. Albany: State University of New York Press, 2015.

Piper-Mandy, Erylene, and Taasogle Daryl Rowe, "Educating African-Centered Psychologists: Toward a Comprehensive Paradigm." *The Journal of African Studies* 3, no. 8 (June 2010). https://www.jpanafrican.org/docs/vol3no8/3.8EducatingAfrican.pdf.

Rifkin, Mark. *Beyond Settler Time: Temporal Sovereignty and Indigenous Self-Determination*. Durham, NC: Duke University Press, 2017.

Robinson, Cedric J. *Black Marxism: The Making of the Black Radical Tradition*, 3rd ed. Chapel Hill: University of North Carolina Press, 2021.

Simpson, Leanne Betasamosake. *As We Have Always Done: Indigenous Freedom through Radical Resistance*. Minneapolis: University of Minnesota Press, 2017.

Somé, Malidoma Patrice. *Ritual: Power, Healing and Community*. New York: Plume, 1997.

Yunkaporta, Tyson. *Sand Talk: How Indigenous Thinking Can Save the World*. Melbourne, Australia: Text Publishing Company, 2023.

INDEX

E

E-40, 142–143
Earth, relationship to, 129, 159–160, 179
echolocation, 45
Eder, 169–170
education
 Eurocentric, 31
 exploring new modes of, 33
 by imagination, 149
 as oppression, 21–22, 167
 whiteness vs. reforms in, 52
elders, 34
Elizabeth II, Queen, 163
Emeryville, California, 85
empathy, 103
enslavement
 and borders, 32–33
 and business practices, 27–29
 maroons' escape from, 106–108
 and prison, 87–88
 refusal to remember, 14, 32
 resistance to, 88
 and whiteness, 49
 and whitewashing of history, 31
entertainment, 23–24
epistemic disobedience, 111
"equity," 109–111
erasure, cultural
 in American education, 31
 assimilation and, 41
 cognitive justice vs., 34
 and forgetting of history, 31, 116
 in missionary/residential schools, 21–22
 of music, 23–24
 of settler colonialism, 162–163
Erylene, Piper-Mandy, 172
Ethiopia
 colonization resisted by, 6–7, 26, 108–109
 culture of dignity in, 63–65
 famine in, 18
 immigrants from, 20
 language of, 167
 philosophers of, 167–168
 sterilization of Jews from, 24–25
 time in, 138

ethnography, 39
eugenics, 24–25
Eurocentricity
 and beauty ideals, 81
 defying, 105
 "history" through the lens of, 30–31
 imposing the mindset of, 71
 superiority doctrine of, 15
 as taught in residentials schools, 21
 and whiteness, 50
experience, lived
 of Africans, 3
 of the author, 6–7
 of colonialism, 2–3, 13–15
 denial of, 30–31
 of incarceration, 92
 knowledge via, 33
 memory of, 34–36
 naming of, 44
 as yours, 76
exploitation
 anthropological/ethnographic, 39–41
 of Black women, 95
 in design industry, 69–73, 103
 of land and labor, 15–17, 160
 via PC buzzwords, 115
 via representation without power, 43
 resistance to. *See* resistance
 rest vs. systems of, 80–81
 via sports, 81–86

F

failure, 71
faith, 96–97
family, 137, 159
Fanon, Frantz, 1, 19, 42
farming, 161–162
fashion, 46–47, 81, 82
fasting, 102
feeling, 124, 125, 130, 172
fiction, 149–151
financial support, 169–170
Finley, Vernon, 40
Floyd, George, 74, 75

ABOUT THE AUTHOR

Author, founder, and organizer Aida Mariam Davis is relentlessly committed to the dignity and distinction of the African and Black way of life. She is part of a long tradition of poets, philosophers, and prophets who participate in liberation movements in the US and abroad. Specifically, she is a descendant of anticolonial fighters who kept Ethiopia free from colonialism when virtually all of Africa was colonized. Her life's work has been to excavate the historical and ongoing impacts of settler colonialism, making explicit the ways in which extraction, oppression, and enslavement serve the goals of empire—not least by severing ancestral connections and disrupting profound and ancient relationships to self, nature, and community.

ABOUT
NORTH ATLANTIC BOOKS

North Atlantic Books (NAB) is an independent, nonprofit publisher committed to a bold exploration of the relationships between mind, body, spirit, and nature. Founded in 1974, NAB aims to nurture a holistic view of the arts, sciences, humanities, and healing. To make a donation or to learn more about our books, authors, events, and newsletter, please visit www.northatlanticbooks.com.